Colossians

Complete in Christ

JOHN A. STEWART

Lamplighters International is a Christian ministry that helps individuals engage with God and His Word and equips believers to be disciple-makers.

For additional information about Lamplighters ministry resources, contact:

Lamplighters International
771 NE Harding Street, Suite 250
Minneapolis, MN USA 55413
or visit our website at
www.LamplightersUSA.org

Product Code Co-NK-2P

ISBN 978-1-931372-66-4

Contents

How to Use This Study

WHAT IS LAMPLIGHTERS?

Lamplighters is a Christian ministry that helps individuals engage with God and His Word and equips believers to be disciple-makers. This Bible study, comprising nine individual lessons, is a self-contained unit and an integral part of the entire discipleship ministry. When you have completed the study, you will have a much greater understanding of a portion of God's Word, with many new truths that you can apply to your life.

HOW TO STUDY A LAMPLIGHTERS LESSON

A Lamplighters study begins with prayer, your Bible, the weekly lesson, and a sincere desire to learn more about God's Word. The questions are presented in a progressive sequence as you work through the study material. You should not use Bible commentaries or other reference books (except a dictionary) until you have completed your weekly lesson and met with your weekly group. Approaching the Bible study in this way allows you to personally encounter many valuable spiritual truths from the Word of God.

To gain the most out of the Bible study, find a quiet place to complete your weekly lesson. Each lesson will take approximately 45–60 minutes to complete. You will likely spend more time on the first few lessons until you are familiar with the format, and our prayer is that each week will bring the discovery of important life principles.

The writing space within the weekly studies provides the opportunity for you to answer questions and respond to what you have learned. Putting answers in your own words, and including Scripture references where appropriate, will help you personalize and commit to memory the truths you have learned. The answers to the questions will be found in the Scripture references at the end of each question or in the passages listed at the beginning of each lesson.

If you are part of a small group, it's a good idea to record the specific dates that you'll be meeting to do the individual lessons. Record the specific dates each time the group will be meeting next to the lesson titles on the Contents page. Additional lines have been provided for you to record when you go through this same study at a later date.

The side margins in the lessons can be used for the spiritual insights you glean from other group or class members. Recording these spiritual truths will likely be a spiritual help to you and others when you go through this study again in the future.

AUDIO INTRODUCTION

A brief audio introduction is available to help you learn about the historical background of the book, gain an understanding of its theme and structure, and be introduced to some of the major truths. Audio introductions are available for all Lamplighters studies and are a great resource for the group leader; they can also be used to introduce the study to your group. To access the audio introductions, go to www.LamplightersUSA.org.

"DO YOU THINK?" QUESTIONS

Each weekly study has a few *"do you think?"* questions designed to help you to make personal applications from the biblical truths you are learning. In the first lesson the *"do you think?"* questions are placed in italic print for easy identification. If you are part of a study group, your insightful answers to these questions could be a great source of spiritual encouragement to others.

PERSONAL QUESTIONS

Occasionally you'll be asked to respond to personal questions. If you are part of a study group you may choose not to share your answers to these questions with the others. However, be sure to answer them for your own benefit because they will help you compare your present level of spiritual maturity to the biblical principles presented in the lesson.

A FINAL WORD

Throughout this study the masculine pronouns are frequently used in the generic sense to avoid awkward sentence construction. When the pronouns *he*, *him*, and *his* are used in reference to the Trinity (God the Father, Jesus Christ, and the Holy Spirit), they always refer to the masculine gender.

This Lamplighters study was written after many hours of careful preparation. It is our prayer that it will help you "… grow in the grace and knowledge of our Lord and Savior Jesus Christ. To Him be the glory both now and forever. Amen" (2 Peter 3:18).

WHAT IS AN INTENTIONAL DISCIPLESHIP BIBLE STUDY?

THE *NEXT STEP* IN BIBLE STUDY

The Lamplighters Bible study series is ideal for individual, small group, and classroom use. This Bible study is also designed for Intentional Discipleship training. An Intentional Discipleship (ID) Bible study has four key components. Individually they are not unique, but together they form the powerful core of the ID Bible study process.

1. Objective: Lamplighters is a discipleship training ministry that has a dual objective: (1) to help individuals engage with God and His Word and (2) to equip believers to be disciple-makers. The small group format provides extensive opportunity for ministry training, and it's not limited by facilities, finances, or a lack of leadership staffing.

2. Content: The Bible is the focus rather than Christian books. Answers to the study questions are included within the study guides, so the theology is in the study material, not in the leader's mind. This accomplishes two key objectives: (1) It gives the group leader confidence to lead another individual or small group without fear, and (2) it protects the small group from theological error.

3. Process: The ID Bible study process begins with an Open House, which is followed by a 6–14-week study, which is followed by a presentation of the Final Exam (see graphic on page 8). This process provides a natural environment for continuous spiritual growth and leadership development.

4. Leadership Development: As group participants grow in Christ, they naturally invite others to the groups. The leader-trainer (1) identifies and recruits new potential leaders from within the group, (2) helps them register for online discipleship training, and (3) provides in-class leadership mentoring until they are both competent and confident to lead a group according to the ID Bible study process. This leadership development process is scalable, progressive, and comprehensive.

Overview of the Leadership Training and Development Process

There are three stages of leadership training in the Intentional Discipleship process: (1) leading studies, (2) training leaders, and (3) multiplying groups (see appendix for greater detail).

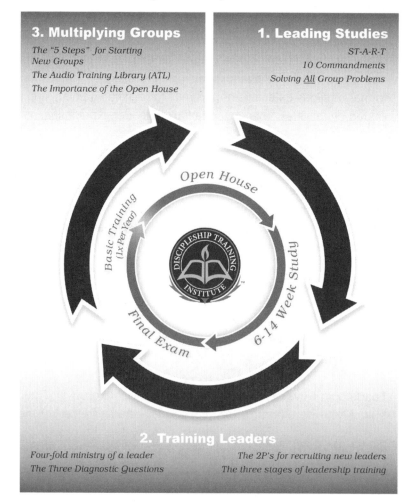

Intentional Discipleship

Training & Development Process

3. Multiplying Groups

The "5 Steps" for Starting New Groups
The Audio Training Library (ATL)
The Importance of the Open House

1. Leading Studies

ST-A-R-T
10 Commandments
Solving All Group Problems

Open House

Basic Training (1x Per Year)

6-14 Week Study

Final Exam

2. Training Leaders

Four-fold ministry of a leader
The Three Diagnostic Questions

The 2P's for recruiting new leaders
The three stages of leadership training

How Can I Be Trained?

Included within this Bible study is the student workbook for Level 1 (Basic Training). Level 1 training is both free and optional. Level 1 training teaches you a simple 4-step process (ST-A-R-T) to help you prepare a life-changing Bible study and 10 proven small group leadership principles that will help your group thrive. To register for a Level 1 online training event, either as an individual or as a small group, go to www.LamplightersUSA.org/training or www.discipleUSA.org. If you have additional questions, you can also call 800-507-9516.

INTRODUCTION

If you are a casual Christian—one that sees your relationship with Christ as primarily a Sunday morning event—you should think twice about studying Colossians. Colossians will challenge your concept of casual Christianity and destroy the fallacy of seeing life as partly spiritual (going to church, reading the Bible) and partly secular (work, finances, etc.). In fact, if you study Colossians, you'll learn there's no such thing as a secular life or secular job for a Christian.

On the other hand, if you really want to grow as a Christian, Colossians will teach you *why* and *how* to give your life to Christ. Colossians is a book that will strengthen your resolve to live wholeheartedly for Christ, and it will show you how to do so in the details of life.

The book begins with a powerful affirmation of the supremacy of Jesus Christ. Then Colossians demonstrates that Christ's supremacy extends over all the earth and over every person, Christian and non-Christian alike (whether they realize or acknowledge it or not). As the doctrine of Christ's supremacy unfolds, profound implications and applications come into view. Your thoughts and attitudes, your work life, as well as marriage and family, are all subject to Christ's supremacy. And living for Christ becomes not another weekend responsibility but a life-transforming experience. Do you see why the Book is a danger to the casual and a comfort to the committed?

BACKGROUND

Both Jews and proselytes (non-Jewish converts to Judaism) heard the apostle Peter preach in Jerusalem on the day of Pentecost (Acts 2:41–43). Among them were worshippers from Phrygia, the Roman province in which the city of Colossae was located (Acts 2:10). It is likely that the early Colossian church consisted of those who were converted to Christ under Peter's preaching and others who were later reached through the apostle Paul's personal missionary efforts.

After Paul's third missionary journey, he was imprisoned in Rome, where he was visited by Epaphras, a leader of the Colossian church (Colossians 1:7). Epaphras brought disturbing news of the church's willingness to embrace heretical teaching. Paul wrote to the Colossian church to warn them against embracing false teaching and to tell them that they had everything they needed in Jesus Christ to become spiritually mature (Colossians 2:9–10).

THE "FOUR THREATS" TO SPIRITUAL MATURITY

The book of Colossians identifies four threats to spiritual growth (worldly philosophies, legalism, mysticism, and asceticism) that threatened to derail the Colossian believers' spiritual growth. Each of the four terms will be defined in the study, and examples will help you identify and avoid these threats to your relationship with Christ.

SPIRITUAL VALUE AND SIGNIFICANCE

The spiritual value of Colossians for the church today is huge. Colossians' bold declaration of Christ's supremacy over all creation challenges the common error that life is comprised of both the secular and the sacred. *Casual* or *worldly Christians* are terms that identify too many within the professing Christian community. Those who study Colossians will be forced to decide whether to yield to Christ's supremacy over all their lives or face the reality of their own spiritual rebellion and its consequences.

Another spiritual benefit of studying Colossians is learning that God cares about your work. Far too many Christians have not understood that God is infinitely concerned about all aspects of your work life. And God's concern goes far beyond productivity to include your attitude and the realization that God, the Great Employer, rewards workplace excellence and impartially recompenses inferior work. But Christ's supremacy is not just about your work life. All aspects of life, including marriage and family life, are to come under the authority of Christ's supremacy. This is the message of Colossians—a life that's fully integrated into Christ.

ONE

THE LIFE-CHANGING GOSPEL

Read Introduction, Colossians 1:1–12; other references as given.

What would happen if you gave your entire life to Jesus Christ? What extraordinary things would God do in you and through you? Evangelist Dwight Moody (1837–1899) said, "The world has yet to see what God would do through a man who was completely surrendered to Him." What if that person was you?

The book of Colossians teaches Christians why we should give our entire lives to Jesus Christ and what our lives would look like when we do. Paul, writing under the inspiration of the Holy Spirit, teaches us in only four short chapters how we can give Christ His rightful place in our lives. Only four chapters, but four chapters that could change your life forever!

In the first lesson Paul affirms his love for the Colossian believers and expresses his desire for their spiritual growth. He emphasizes the fact that the gospel—the truth that changed their lives—continues to change lives throughout the world. His point? The gospel of Jesus Christ is enough for all believers, for all the world, for all time. Adding to God's Word doesn't strengthen it. It distorts the truth and leads believers into error.

Now ask God to reveal Himself to you through His Word and conform you into the image of Jesus Christ.

1. Paul introduced himself as **an apostle of Jesus Christ by the will of God** (Colossians 1:1). He included Timothy, missionary companion and spiritual brother, in his initial

Lombardi Time Rule:

If the leader arrives early, he or she has time to pray, prepare the room, and greet others personally.

ADD GROUP INSIGHTS BELOW

greeting to the church. What words are used to describe the Colossian Christians (Colossians 1:2)?

_____

_____

_____

2. When the word *saint* is applied to the New Testament believer, it signifies our dual calling to salvation and sanctification (1 Corinthians 1:2). Alexander MacLean, a famous Scottish preacher, said, "Saints are not an eminent sort of Christian, but all Christians are saints, and he who is not a saint is not a Christian." What are some other words the Bible uses to describe the believer's relationship to God (John 1:12; Galatians 4:5, 7; 1 Peter 2:9)?

1. _____ (_____)

2. _____ (_____)

3. _____ (_____)

4. _____ (_____)

5. _____ (_____)

6. _____ (_____)

7. _____ (_____)

3. a. Paul often expressed thankfulness for other believers (Romans 1:8; 1 Corinthians1:4; Philippians 1:3). What specific spiritual qualities was he particularly thankful for in the lives of the Colossian believers (Colossians 1:3–4)?

    _____

    _____

    b. Name two things Paul did to express his gratitude for the Colossians:

        1. _____

        _____ .

2. _____

_____ .

c. In what ways have you *recently* expressed your appreciation and gratitude for another Christian?

_____

_____

Zip-It Rule:

Group members should agree to disagree, but should never be disagreable.

———

ADDITIONAL INSIGHTS

4. a. The Colossian church had a love for **all the saints** (Colossians 1:4). The remarkable frequency of the word **all** (28 times in only 95 verses) is more than coincidence. It emphasizes an important truth. Please list the remaining phrases that include the word **all** and their corresponding verse references in Colossians 1.

_____ (v. ____)

_____ (v. ____)

_____ (v. ____)

_____ (v. ____)

_____ (v. ____)

_____ (v. ____)

_____ (v. ____)

b. What important spiritual truth *do you think* is being taught by the frequent use of the word **all** when it is linked together with the other terms?

_____

_____

_____

5. The Christian traits of faith, love, and hope form a familiar triad (trio) in Scripture (Romans 5:2–5; 1 Corinthians 13:13; 1 Thessalonians 1:3; 5:8). In these passages, hope is coordinated with faith and love, but in Colossians 1:4–5

hope represents the source from which faith and love spring. What *do you think* is meant by the phrase **the hope which is laid up for you in heaven** (Colossians 1:5)?

_____

_____

_____

_____

_____

_____

6. a. What was Paul referring to in Colossians 1:6 when he said, **which has come to you, as it has also in all the world, and is bringing forth fruit?**

_____

_____

  b. The phrase, **which has come to you, as it has also in all the world, and is bringing forth fruit,** has profound theological implications, especially in the area of world missions. What *do you think* this important phrase teaches about the spread of the gospel (the good news of salvation by grace through faith in Jesus Christ alone) throughout the world?

_____

_____

_____

_____

7. a. Bible scholars believe God used Epaphras to start the church at Colossae (Colossians 1:7; note: Epaphras is a shortened form of Epaphroditus, but this man should not be identified with the man by the same name in Philippians 2:25 and 4:18). Paul was obviously

impressed with Epaphras's spiritual character. How did Paul describe this man (Colossians 1:7)?

_____

_____

Want to learn how to disciple another person, lead a life-changing Bible study or start another study? Go to www.Lamplighters USA.org/training to learn how.

————

ADDITIONAL INSIGHTS

b. Sometimes we view the biblical characters as otherworldly—people we read about, but whose lives could never be replicated. The truth is, however, that they were ordinary people who simply surrendered their lives to Christ and allowed Him to work through them for God's glory. What aspects of your life would you need to surrender more fully to Christ to become a **dear fellow servant, who is a faithful minister of Christ**?

_____

_____

_____

8. Paul thanked God for the Colossian Christians (Colossians 1:3) and then offered a specific request on their behalf. What was it (Colossians 1:9)?

_____

_____

_____

9. Some Christians are uncertain what God wants from their lives (God's will). They appear to wander aimlessly in their Christian lives, unsure how they can serve God. List four specific things God desires every Christian to do to fulfill His will (Colossians 1:10–12).

1. _____

   _____ (v. _____)

2. _____

   _____ (v. _____)

3. _____

_____ (v. _____)

4. _____

_____ (v. _____)

Two

The Supremacy of Christ

**Read Colossians 1:13–23;
other references as given.**

Does the Bible teach that believing (trusting) in Jesus Christ alone for salvation is enough? The answer is yes. But is Christ enough for sanctification—the process of spiritual growth by which the believer progressively surrenders to Christ's lordship and learns to live a God-glorifying life? That's a different question.

In this lesson the apostle Paul presents one of the most complete passages in the entire Bible on the sufficiency of Jesus Christ. Words and phrases such as **"He," "in whom," "in Him," "through Him,"** are repeated to emphasize Christ's supremacy over this world, including your life. Paul's point? Everything Jesus offers us in salvation is ours, but it must be accepted by faith. And everything we are, or ever will be, belongs to Christ.

Now ask God to reveal Himself to you through His Word and conform you into the image of Jesus Christ.

Volunteer Rule:

If the leader asks for volunteers to read, pray, and answer the questions, group members will be more inclined to invite newcomers.

ADD GROUP
INSIGHTS BELOW

1. Only Christians can share in a future inheritance God promises to those who have **been transferred from the power** [or domain] **of darkness into the kingdom** of Jesus Christ (Colossians 1:12–13).

    a. Several important truths regarding man's salvation are taught in Colossians 1:13. Please name at least three.

       1. _____

       _____ .

2. _____

_____ .

3. _____

_____ .

4. _____

_____ .

b. Before an individual is saved, he is a servant of sin and a child of wrath (Romans 6:20; Ephesians 2:3). When an individual is saved by grace through faith in Christ alone (Romans 10:9–10, 13), he or she is transferred to the authority of Jesus Christ (Colossians 1:13). How is an individual described after salvation (2 Corinthians 5:17, 20; Philippians 3:20)?

_____

_____

_____

2. In Colossians 1:13 Paul begins an active assault on the theological error that had crept into the Colossian church. The Colossian heresy was a mixture of ritualism (religious rules without biblical basis [often called legalism]), philosophical rationalism (human reason that denies the reality of God [modern-day liberalism and humanism]), and pagan mysticism (experience-centered religiosity). The false teachers offered these heresies as a higher form of wisdom or enlightenment and were attempting to undermine the Colossian believers' confidence with regard to Christ's deity (Colossians 1:15a), creation (Colossians 1:15b–17) and the church (Colossians 1:18).

a. Christ is **the image of the invisible God** (Colossians 1:15). What do you think this means (John 1:18; Hebrews 1:3)?

_____

_____

_____

_____

_____

b. In the phrase **the firstborn** (Colossians 1:15, 18), the Greek word *prototokos* can mean "first in time" or "first in rank." Do you think this statement means first in time, first in rank (supremacy), or both (Colossians 1:15–18)?

_____

_____

3. a. Give three reasons why Christ has the right to be the supreme ruler over all creation, including mankind (Colossians 1:16–17).

1. _____ (v. _____)

2. _____ (v. _____)

3. _____ (v. _____)

b. Christ is the rightful ruler over all creation, including you. In what area or areas of your life, if any, do you still struggle to yield to His lordship (life goals, values, habits, thoughts and attitudes, relationships, finances, etc.)?

_____

_____

_____

4. Paul said **in Him all things consist** (Colossians 1:17; NIV: "hold together"). What do you think this means?

_____

_____

_____

59:59 Rule:

Participants appreciate when the leader starts and finishes the studies on time—all in one hour (the 59:59 rule). If the leader doesn't complete the entire lesson, the participants will be less likely to do their weekly lessons and the Bible study discussion will tend to wander.

———

ADDITIONAL INSIGHTS

5. Paul's third affirmation of Christ's supremacy over all creation includes the church. In Colossians 1:18 Paul states that Christ is **the head of the body, the church, who is the beginning, the firstborn from the dead, that in all things he may have the preeminence.**

a. If you are a Christian, you are the church! How do you manifest Christ's preeminence in your life?

_____

_____

_____

_____

b. The word *church* also refers to local, organized assemblies of believers. What are some things churches do that indicate they are *not* acknowledging Jesus Christ's supremacy in their ministries?

1. _____

_____ .

2. _____

_____ .

3. _____

_____ .

4. _____

_____ .

6. The Colossian heretics taught that an individual acquired truth by means of subjective enlightenment. But the Bible teaches that truth comes objectively through a person, Jesus Christ (note: there are 17 references to Christ in Colossians 1:15–20 that emphasize this truth, **in Him, through Him, by him,** etc.). What do you think is meant by the statement, **it pleased the Father that in Him all the fullness should dwell** (Colossians 1:19)?

_____

_____

_____

_____

35% Rule:

If the leader talks
more than 35% of
the time, the group
members will be
less likely
to participate.

ADDITIONAL
INSIGHTS

7. a. Man is rescued from the domain of darkness by Jesus Christ; not intellectual enlightenment or subjective experience (Colossians 1:13–14). How is man, who is alienated from God and hostile toward Him, actually delivered or saved from his desperate spiritual state prior to salvation (Colossians 1:20–23; John 3:36)?

_____

_____

_____

_____

b. Are you certain that you have been rescued from the domain of darkness and transferred into the kingdom of Jesus Christ? To say it another way, have you been saved (born again) according to God's Holy Word?

_____

When and where did that happen?

_____

_____

If you are not sure what it means to be born again, or you are not sure if that has even happened in your life, read the Final Exam in the back of this study book. It will explain how you can be born again according to the Bible.

ADDITIONAL INSIGHTS

Three

Standing with Christ

Read Colossians 1:24–29; other references as given.

New Age followers view "God" as an abstract principle, universal mind, or cosmic force or energy that mystically and progressively elevates man to new heights of spiritual enlightenment. They are reluctant to use the terms *divine being* or *personality* because they imply a personal god who demands ultimate accountability. They take a smorgasbord approach to spirituality that allows them to embrace a personal concept of spiritual enlightenment, but one that ignores the cross and carefully avoids God's essential attributes of holiness and righteousness.

But Jesus Christ is not an abstract principle, an impersonal mind, or a mystical force. Jesus Christ is God who became a man, entered a sinful world, suffered on a piece of wood He created, and reconciled all things to Himself (Colossians 1:20). Christ's authority extends over all creation, including mankind. In this lesson the apostle Paul explains that the gospel was promised long ago and has been fully revealed only now, in these last days. In this lesson you'll learn why it is so important to stand up for the truth.

Now ask God to reveal Himself to you through His Word and conform you into the image of Jesus Christ.

1. In what ways did Paul demonstrate Christ's authority over his life (Colossians 1:24; 2 Timothy 1:8)?

Focus Rule:

If the leader helps the group members focus on the Bible, they will gain confidence to study God's Word on their own.

ADD GROUP INSIGHTS BELOW

25

_____

_____

2. Many Christians rejoice when God blesses their lives, but they find it difficult to praise Him during their trials. But Paul considered it a privilege to suffer for Christ and he rejoiced during his sufferings as a prisoner (Colossians 1:24).

    a. Paul knew two important spiritual truths that helped him to rejoice in his sufferings rather than grumble or complain about his situation. What are they (Colossians 1:16–18)?

        1. _____

            _____ (v. _____)

        2. _____

            _____ (v. _____)

    b. Now think of a troubling situation in your life over which you have little or no control (family, financial, work problem, relationship, etc.). What specific things do you think you could do to bring more glory to God during the trial?

        1. _____

            _____ .

        2. _____

            _____ .

3. Although many believers would not consider prison an effective place for ministry, Paul continued to serve God faithfully (Colossians 1:24). List five things Paul did to serve the Lord in prison (Colossians 1:1–3, 9; Acts 16:25, 28–32; 2 Timothy 4:13).

    1. _____

        _____ (_____)

2. _____

_____ (_____)

3. _____

_____ (_____)

4. _____

_____ (_____)

5. _____

_____ (_____)

Drawing Rule:

To learn how to draw everyone into the group discussion without calling on anyone, go to www.Lamplighters USA.org/training.

———

ADDITIONAL INSIGHTS

4. The difficult phrase, **fill up what is lacking in the afflictions of Christ,** has been the topic of much debate (Colossians 1:24). Some interpret the "afflictions" of Christ as Christ's redemptive sufferings on the cross and believe all true followers of Christ must suffer with Him to complete the work of redemption (salvation).

a. How can we be sure Colossians 1:24 does *not* teach this theological perspective (Colossians 2:12–13; John 19:30; Hebrews 10:10–12)?

_____

_____

_____

b. If the phrase **fill up in my flesh what is lacking in the afflictions of Christ** does not refer to salvation, what do you think it means?

_____

_____

_____

_____

_____

5. Paul was commissioned by God to be a **minister** (Greek *diakonos*—minister, servant, deacon) to the church (Colossians 1:25). One of his responsibilities was to equip God's people by preaching the Word of God (Colossians 1:25).

a. What word or phrase indicates Paul fully understood and accepted Christ's supremacy and authority in this particular area of his life (Colossians 1:25)?

_____

b. Paul verbally acknowledged Christ's authority over his life to an entire church (Colossians 1:25). Have you acknowledged Christ's supremacy and authority over your life to God and yourself, ... to your spouse, ... to your friends, ... to your co-workers and even strangers?

_____

If you haven't, why not acknowledge Jesus Christ's authority over every aspect of your life right now?

_____

Do you realize that sharing God's Word with others is a stewardship responsibility for which you will eventually give account to God (Mark 16:15; Romans 14:12)?

_____

6. The real **mystery** (Gk. *musterion*—mystery, secret; used in the New Testament of truth as undiscoverable except through divine revelation; 1 Corinthians 2:6–10) of God is available to all who will come to Christ in faith (Colossians 1:26: **saints**). If the mystery of God is not some secret spiritual enlightenment, what is the mystery that God has revealed to believers (Colossians 1:26–27)?

_____

_____

_____

_____

_____

Has your group become a "Holy huddle?" Learn how to reach out to others by taking online leadership training.

_____

ADDITIONAL INSIGHTS

7. The Colossian heretics taught that a "mystery" was a secret teaching known only to an exclusive group and unknowable to the masses. Only those who were initiated by certain "anointed" leaders were able to become enlightened by the truth. In contrast to the secretive methods of the false teachers, Paul and his followers preached (Gk. *kataggello*— declare, proclaim publicly, publish) Christ's message to everyone who would listen (Colossians 1:28).

a. The false teachers' objective or agenda was to ensnare naive followers who would be dependent upon them. What was Paul and the other missionaries' objective for preaching Jesus Christ (Colossians 1:28)?

_____

_____

_____

b. What did they do to accomplish their goal (Colossians 1:28–29)?

_____

_____

_____

c. If you are a Christian, in what ways do you strive to see others come to Christ and understand the riches of His glory?

_____

_____

_____

8. The Colossian church had been easily seduced by false religious leaders who claimed they possessed a special, spiritual anointing and promised their faithful followers spiritual enlightenment. Even today many within the church continue to be easy prey for spiritual entrapment. Pastor Charles Haddon Spurgeon said, "Christ's faithful servants are to follow His example, to quarrel with error, to fight against sin, to be aggressive against everything that is opposed to our Lord and His truth." What could you do to take a stronger stand for the truth and be less susceptible to spiritual deception?

_____

_____

_____

_____

_____

FOUR

WALKING IN CHRIST

Read Colossians 2:1–7; other references as given.

The gospel of Jesus Christ has been changing lives for hundreds of years. It has been saving souls, reclaiming broken lives, restoring hope, giving peace, and providing complete assurance of eternal acceptance before a holy God. The gospel is not an abstract truth—it's the revelation of the person of Jesus Christ. It was promised long ago through the prophets but was only revealed (in its full expression through Jesus Christ) in these last days.

In Colossians 2 Paul begins to confront the Colossian believers with the"four errors." Before Paul identifies the four doctrinal errors that threatened their (and our) spiritual lives, he reaffirms his love for them and reiterates that Christ is sufficient to make them all God wants them to be. In this lesson the Bible teaches the secret to walking with Christ so you can avoid the spiritual traps that threaten your spiritual progress.

Now ask God to reveal Himself to you through His Word and conform you into the image of Jesus Christ.

Gospel Gold Rule:

Try to get all the answers to the questions—not just the easy ones. Go for the gold.

ADD GROUP
INSIGHTS BELOW

1. The lordship of Christ led Paul to suffer as a prisoner (Colossians 1:24; 4:10, 18) and to work tirelessly for the salvation of others (Colossians 1:28–29). A third aspect of Paul's ministry was his constant concern for the believers' spiritual growth in all the churches (Colossians 2:1; 2 Corinthians 11:28). What do you think was the conflict or struggle Paul experienced on behalf of the churches at

Colossae and Laodicea and some other believers whom he had never met (Colossians 2:1–2)?

_____

_____

2. What things did Paul want to see God accomplish in their lives (Colossians 2:2)?

1. _____

_____ .

2. _____

_____ .

3. _____

_____ .

3. Some Christians believe that consistent fellowship with other believers is an option to be considered rather than a command to be obeyed (Hebrews 10:24–25). Their inconsistent fellowship with other believers hinders their spiritual growth, makes them a stumbling block to new believers, and often causes them to be unaware of the spiritual, emotional, and physical needs of others within the church. What are some spiritual benefits of being closely connected in Christian fellowship with other believers (Colossians 2:2)?

1. _____

_____ .

2. _____

_____ .

3. _____

_____ .

4. _____

_____ .

4. The Colossian heretics taught their followers that divine truth was acquired only through their spiritual instruction. As a result, their followers naturally developed an unhealthy addiction toward these false leaders.

a. Where should all Christians look to find the knowledge of God (Colossians 2:2–3)?

_____

_____

b. Why should all Christians worship God alone (Matthew 4:10; Acts 17:29; Romans 1:22–23)?

1. _____

_____ (_____).

2. _____

_____ (_____).

3. _____

_____ (_____).

5. What are some things Christians (and unsaved religious people) worship in place of God (Romans 1:25; Acts 12:21–23; 19:24–27)?

_____

_____

_____

6. In 2 Timothy 3:7 the Bible says some men are **always learning and never able to come to the knowledge of the truth**. It has been said that "atheism denies truth, agnosticism doubts truth, rationalism questions truth, hedonism mocks truth, and secularism gropes for truth."

a. What two things did Jesus say about truth (John 14:6; 17:17)?

Balance Rule:

To learn how to balance the group discussion, go to www.Lamplighters USA.org/training.

———

ADDITIONAL INSIGHTS

1. _____

_____ (_____).

2. _____

_____ (_____).

b. If you are a Christian, are you absolutely convinced that Jesus Christ is the complete embodiment of the truth, the complete revelation of God the Father, and the complete revelation of God as revealed in His Holy Bible?

_____

_____

7. Even though many Christians know that the source of all wisdom and knowledge is Jesus Christ, they struggle to make Christ a living reality in their lives. They see Christ either as a hard taskmaster who is ready to give them an endless list of spiritual responsibilities or as a benevolent grandfather who loves all and forgives all.

a. In the statement **as you therefore have received Christ Jesus the Lord, so walk in Him** (Colossians 2:6), there are at least two important spiritual truths that will help every believer in his relationship with Christ. What are they (Colossians 2:6; John 15:5)?

1. _____

_____

_____ (_____).

2. _____

_____

_____ (_____).

b. Paul's frequent use of the word **walk** (Colossians 1:10; 2:6; Gk. *peripateo*—to walk, to conduct one's life in a certain way) suggests a continuous manner of living and the need to keep in stride with the one you are walking with. What must a Christian do to fulfill this command (Colossians 2:7)?

_____

_____

_____

8. The Bible uses several common words from everyday life to teach profound spiritual truths about the believer's relationship to God. Each of the following terms and verse references has been carefully selected, and an appropriate definition has been presented. Match the term on the left with the corresponding definition by drawing a line to the correct answer.

1. Sit (Ephesians 2:6)	refers to the Christian's need to live by faith after salvation and to be led by the Holy Spirit.
2. Rest (Hebrews 4:9–10)	refers to the believer's responsibility to remain loyal to Christ in times of adversity through the power of the Holy Spirit.
3. Walk (Colossians 2:6)	refers to the believer's need for passion, purpose, endurance, and single-mindedness in his or her devotion to Christ.
4. Run (Hebrews 12:1)	refers to the believer's present and eternal standing before God as a result of Jesus' finished work on his or her behalf.
5. Stand (Ephesians 6:14)	refers to the peace a believer can possess if he or she learns to trust fully in God's promises.

If the leader places a watch on the table, participants will feel confident that the Bible study will be completed on time. If the leader doesn't complete the lesson each week, participants will be less likely to do their weekly lessons, and the discussion will not be as rich.

———

ADDITIONAL INSIGHTS

9. Now review each of the terms listed above and their brief definition. Which ones, if any, have you found to be most difficult to comprehend and appropriate into your life?

_____

_____

_____

_____

_____

FIVE

REJECT WORLDLY PHILOSOPHIES

Read Colossians 2:8–10; 1 Corinthians 1:18–31; other references as given.

In the previous lesson you were introduced to the secret of living a God-honoring life. Living by faith is God's plan for every believer and the very essence of the Christian life He wants every believer to experience. You were also introduced to four additional key words—*sit*, *rest*, *run*, *stand*—each one representing an important aspect of successful Christian living.

In this lesson Paul addresses the first of four spiritual threats to draw you away from Christ. Each of the four errors offers an attractive alternative to walking by faith. In this lesson you will also learn the difference between the wisdom of God and the wisdom of man and what you must do to stand strong for Christ. You will study a key passage in 1 Corinthians that will help you understand the wisdom of man and why it can threaten your Christian life.

Now ask God to reveal Himself to you through His Word and conform you into the image of Jesus Christ.

No-Trespassing Rule:

To keep the Bible study on track, avoid talking about political parties, church denominations, and Bible translations.

ADD GROUP INSIGHTS BELOW

1. The first error taught by the false teachers at Colossae was false philosophy (Colossians 2:8). The word **philosophy** (Gk. *philosophia*—love of wisdom) can be used either positively (a love of the wisdom of God) or negatively (a love for the wisdom of man; cf. James 3:13–16). In Scripture, "the wisdom of man" refers to man-centered, secular philosophies that sound true, but actually contradict God's Word (1 Corinthians 1:20–25).

37

a. List three characteristics of these false philosophies that make them particularly dangerous to Christians (Colossians 2:8).

1. _____

_____ .

2. _____

_____ .

3. _____

_____ .

b. How were the Colossian believers to protect themselves against this spiritual danger (Colossians 2:8)?

_____

_____

_____

_____

2. You may be wondering what are some examples of false philosophies that contradict God's Word. Perhaps you have heard someone say, "Man is basically good." This is more than a misguided statement about the nature of man. It is a philosophical statement with significant sociological implications (eternal salvation, welfare, education, etc.) that directly contradicts God's Word (Romans 3:10–12; Ephesians 2:1). List four more false philosophies that also contradict God's Word.

1. _____

_____ .

2. _____

_____ .

3. _____

_____ .

4. _____

    _____ .

3. In 1 Corinthians 1:18–25, the Bible uses the phrase "the wisdom of this world" to refer to humanistic ideas that contradict God's Word. In this passage the Bible compared "the wisdom of man" to "the wisdom of God" to show the superiority of God's wisdom. List three things that Paul says about "the wisdom of man" (1 Corinthians 1:20–25).

    1. _____

        _____ (v. ____)

    2. _____

        _____ (v. ____)

    3. _____

        _____ (v. ____)

4. a. The Old Testament king Solomon pursued several false worldly philosophies in an attempt to find ultimate meaning in life. What was Solomon's assessment of his pursuit of pleasure as the ultimate meaning of life (Ecclesiastes 2:1–2)?

    _____

    b. How did Solomon assess his pursuit of wealth and personal achievement for selfish reasons as the ultimate meaning of life (Ecclesiastes 2:4–11)?

    _____

    _____

    c. How did Solomon assess worldly pleasure and the accumulation of worldly knowledge (Ecclesiastes 2:12–16)?

    _____

    _____

If you use table tents or name tags, it will help visitors feel more comfortable and new members will be assimilated more easily into your group.

ADDITIONAL INSIGHTS

d. What truth did Solomon discover at the end of his quest to find ultimate meaning in life (Ecclesiastes 12:13–14)? Have you discovered this same truth about the whole purpose of living?

_____

_____

_____

_____

5. Why should believers trust God's Word rather than false worldly philosophies when they contradict God's Word (Isaiah 55:8–9)?

_____

_____

6. Many of the world's false philosophies sound so appealing that they are readily embraced by society in general ("All religions are basically the same"; "A loving God would not send anyone to hell").

a. The Bible uses military terminology to describe the fierce battle believers must wage if they hope to be victorious over false worldly philosophies (Ephesians 6:10–17; 2 Corinthians 10:3–5). What did Paul do when false philosophies crept into his own thinking (2 Corinthians 10:4–5)?

_____

_____

_____

b. What does Paul's aggressive approach to rid himself of the false worldly philosophies teach you about how to deal with your own errant thinking?

_____

Use the side margins to write down spiritual insights from other people in your group. Add the person's name and the date to help you remember in the future.

ADDITIONAL INSIGHTS

_____

_____

c. When ungodly thoughts come into your mind, thoughts (really lies) that could take you captive, do you regularly take them captive to the authority of God's Word?

_____

_____

_____

7. The secular philosophies of this world are empty and hollow because they are based upon the false reasoning of fallen men who don't understand the fear of the Lord (Proverbs 1:7; 9:10). Paul contrasts the insufficiency of these humanistic philosophies with the sufficiency of Christ (Colossians 2:8–10). What do you think is meant by the phrase, **you are complete in Him** (Colossians 2:10; John 1:16)?

_____

_____

_____

_____

_____

8. Sometimes believers do not feel **complete in Him** because their minds continue to be occupied with sinful thoughts. They have eternal life, but they still have earthly (unsanctified) minds.

a. List three things every believer must do to cleanse himself from unsanctified (sinful) thoughts so he can know that he is **complete in Christ** (Romans 12:1–2).

1. _____

_____

2. _____

3. _____

_____

b. Sometimes Christians are confused about what it means to present their bodies as a living sacrifice to God. How did Paul fulfill this command, and how did he view himself afterward (Galatians 2:20; Ephesians 3:1, 7)?

_____

_____

_____

_____

Six

Dangerous Detours

In the last lesson Paul identified the first spiritual deception every Christian must avoid—worldly philosophies that contradict God's Word. He said Christians must wage war against all thoughts that contradict God's Word and take them captive to the obedience to Christ (2 Corinthians 10:4–5).

In this lesson Paul confronts the Colossians with three additional errors that threatened their spiritual growth—legalism, mysticism, and asceticism. *Legalism* is defined as a strict, literal, or excessive adherence to a law or religious or moral code. *Mysticism* is the belief that direct knowledge of God or spiritual truth is attained through subjective experience rather than through God's Word. *Asceticism* is the practice of strict personal self-denial with the goal of controlling the appetites of the sinful nature in an attempt to gain favor with God. In this lesson you'll learn why these three errors must be avoided and how to reject them.

Now ask God to reveal Himself to you through His Word and to transform you into the image of Jesus Christ.

Transformation
Rule:

Seek for personal
transformation,
not mere
information, from
God's Word.

———

ADD GROUP
INSIGHTS BELOW

1. The second spiritual attack on the Colossian church was legalism (Colossians 2:11–17). In Colossians 2:11, the abrupt and unexpected reference to circumcision suggests that Paul may be replying to a claim by the false teachers that it is necessary (Colossians 2:11). To accept circumcision as an adult on religious grounds meant a believer was placing

himself under the complete authority of the entire Old Testament Mosaic Law (the specific legal code God gave Moses on Mount Sinai).

What do the following verses teach about the Christian's relationship to the Old Testament Mosaic Law?

1. Romans 6:14: _____

_____

2. Romans 10:4: _____

_____

_____

3. Galatians 3:19–25: _____

_____

_____

2. Legalism entraps believers not by subtracting from the cross but by adding man-made traditions to it. Legalism doubts Christ's ability to save or sanctify the believer by grace alone. It teaches that Jesus Christ is good, but other things must be added if you are "really serious" about following God. These things are always extra-biblical, religious traditions of men that inevitably become the focus of the individual's spiritual attention, the basis for spiritual (or denominational) pride, and an arbitrary standard for judging others.

a. What are some examples of nonbiblical, man-made religious traditions that are not found in God's Word?

1. _____

_____

2. _____

_____

3. _____

_____

4. _____

_____

Would you like to learn how to prepare a life-changing Bible study using a simple 4-step process? Contact Lamplighters and ask about ST-A-R-T.

————

ADDITIONAL
INSIGHTS

b. No legalist thinks he is a legalist, but that's part of his deception! What religious beliefs, if any, do you believe that are not taught in God's Word?

_____

_____

_____

_____

What do you think you should do regarding these man-made beliefs if you expect to become mature in Christ?

_____

_____

3. a. What did Paul tell the Colossian Christians regarding their need for circumcision and keeping the Mosaic Law (Colossians 2:11–12)?

_____

_____

_____

b. What do you think is the meaning of the phrase **you were also circumcised with the circumcision made without hands** (Colossians 2:11; Romans 2:28–29)? (Note: The word *Jew* in this context refers to a true Jew and also someone one converted to Jesus Christ.)

_____

4. Some Christians continue to be plagued with doubts about their relationship with Christ. This lack of assurance robs them of the joy Christ wants them to experience and greatly hinders their effectiveness in His service.

a. What does the Bible say about Christ's work of redemption that should bring joy and assurance to the heart of every believer (Colossians 2:11–15)?

_____

_____

_____

_____

b. Has Christ canceled the **handwriting of requirements that was against us**—against you? Have you trusted Christ alone for everlasting life, or are you trusting in anything else to save you (Romans 10:9–10, 13)?

_____

_____

_____

5. The third danger, mysticism, appeals to the fleshly nature of Christians who want to experience the presence of God, but without committing themselves to a diligent study of the Word (Romans 10:17).

a. While mysticism promises a closer relationship with God, it actually draws people away from Christ (Colossians 2:18–19). What are other negative results of this doctrinal error (Colossians 2:18–19)?

_____

_____

_____

_____

_____

b. What are some examples of modern religious mysticism?

1. _____

2. _____

_____

_____

3. _____

_____

Having trouble
with your group?
A Lamplighters
trainer can help
you solve the
problem.

———

ADDITIONAL
INSIGHTS

6. The Colossian heretics taught a fourth theological error—asceticism (pronounced *a-SET-e-siz-em*). Asceticism is the practice of strict self-denial as a measure of personal and spiritual discipline. Throughout the centuries various religious groups have adopted difficult and even painful restrictions (severe treatment of the body; Colossians 2:20–23) as a means of gaining control over the sinful desires of the body or a means of paying for your sins.

a. Why do you think religious asceticism appears to be a legitimate method of controlling the fleshly desires of the sin nature (Colossians 2:23)?

_____

_____

_____

_____

b. What does the Bible teach about the effectiveness of this method of spiritual growth (Colossians 2:23)?

_____

_____

7. It is possible that the study of these four doctrinal errors has caused you to think seriously about your relationship with Christ and your spiritual growth. Take a moment to honestly evaluate the four errors discussed in this study (worldly human philosophies, legalism, mysticism, and asceticism).

a. Is there one of these four errors that you find easy to accept as truth? Why?

_____

_____

_____

b. What spiritual advice would you give another Christian who has allowed himself to adopt one or more of these four errors which was hindering his or her spiritual growth?

_____

_____

_____

_____

_____

SEVEN

FROM RAGS TO RICHES

Read Colossians 3:1–11; other references as given.

In the previous two lessons you learned about four threats to your spiritual growth (worldly philosophies, legalism, mysticism, asceticism). But spiritual growth is not just an endless list of prohibitions—even though some believers seem to think so ("Don't do this or that"; "Good Christians never go there, or do ..."; "If you want to be a good Christian, you shouldn't ...").

In Colossians 3 and 4 the doctrine of Christ's supremacy is applied to the various aspects of Christian living. Beginning in Colossians 3:1 Paul teaches the Colossian believers how to establish the proper focus on the Christ life. Only when a Christian adopts a God-centered, eternal focus is he or she able to see the world from the right perspective and become an effective witness for Christ.

In this lesson Paul also emphasizes the Christian's need to turn away from the old life and fully embrace new life in Christ. He illustrates this spiritual transformation by comparison with a person discarding filthy clothes (sinful ways) and putting on clean clothes (obedience to Christ or righteous living). This vivid image emphasizes the believer's responsibility to acknowledge Christ's supremacy over every aspect of his life.

Now ask God to reveal Himself to you through His Word and to transform you into the image of Jesus Christ.

1. The great doctrines of the Bible (Christ's supremacy, God's sovereignty, man's depravity, redemption, etc.) are not

Is your study going well? Consider starting a new group. To learn how, go to www. Lamplighters USA.org/training.

———

ADD GROUP INSIGHTS BELOW

merely intellectual puzzles for the spiritually inclined. These truths become the foundation for all that the believer is, or ever will be in Christ. In Colossians 3:1 the word **then** (Gk. *oun*—therefore, then) indicates that Christ's supremacy over all things should be the motivation for the exhortations that follow.

a. If a person has been saved (been raised with Christ), what should he be doing (Colossians 3:1)?

_____

_____

b. What do you think a Christian must do to fulfill the command to **seek those things which are above**?

_____

_____

_____

2. The commands to **seek those things which are above** (Colossians 3:1) and **set your affection on things above** (Colossians 3:2 KJV) are similar, yet distinct. What do you think is the difference between these two commands?

_____

_____

_____

_____

3. As a believer, you are supposed to **set your affection on things above, not on things on the earth** (Colossians 3:2 KJV). How can a Christian fulfill this command in a physical world that seems to require his constant focus and attention (1 Corinthians 10:31–33)?

_____

_____

_____

_____

4. In Colossians 3:5 Paul speaks strongly about God's will for the Christian to live victoriously over the passions of the flesh. One biblical commentator said, "The old life is dead; let it die."

    a. List the specific sins over which Christ has given victory to every Christian, including you (Colossians 3:5).

        1. _____

        2. _____

        3. _____

        4. _____

        5. _____

    b. The phrase **lived in them** (Colossians 3:7) refers to the time prior to salvation when an individual's life was dominated by a desire to fulfill the evil practices mentioned in Colossians 3:5. If you are a Christian, do you have consistent victory over these specific sins?

        _____

        _____

        _____

    c. To what is the sin of **covetousness** compared (Colossians 3:5)? _____
        If an individual is coveting anything (position, possessions, etc.), what does that make him or her?

        _____

        _____

        _____

It's time to choose your next study. Turn to the back of the study guide for a list of available studies or go online for the latest studies.

———

ADDITIONAL
INSIGHTS

5. The first catalog of sins addresses the Christian's need to remove himself from the sins of the flesh (Colossians 3:5). The second list focuses attention on the sins of the believer's attitude and speech (Colossians 3:8).

a. What word does Paul use to emphasize *when* a Christian should rid himself of these sins (Colossians 3:8)?

_____

b. The imagery of the phrase **put off all these** (Gk. *apotithemi*—to lay aside, to put off) is that of putting off clothes—like stripping off soiled and filthy garments. Instead of putting off filthy garments, what sins are Christians to put off (Colossians 3:8–9)?

1. _____ (V. _____)

2. _____ (V. _____)

3. _____ (V. _____)

4. _____ (V. _____)

5. _____ (V. _____)

6. _____ (V. _____)

6. The word **now"** in Colossians 3:8 seems abrupt, but it teaches an important truth about how to overcome sin in your life. Many counselors, including some Christian counselors, believe overcoming a destructive (sinful) habit will likely take months and even years of therapy.

a. What did Jesus instruct the woman caught in adultery to do and when was she to stop her sinful ways (John 8:4–11)?

_____

_____

_____

_____

b. What does the Bible teach Christians about overcoming sin in their lives?

1. 1 Corinthians 10:13: _____

_____

2. 1 John 3:8: _____

_____

It's a good time to begin praying and inviting new people for your next Open House.

ADDITIONAL INSIGHTS

7. Many of God's people struggle in their relationship with Christ because they have never understood the biblical basis for victorious Christian living, which is abiding in Christ or walking in the Spirit. They are busy "doing Christianity" rather than allowing Christ to live through them (John 15:5). Their lives are often marked by guilt, a judgmental or critical spirit, and a preoccupation with only negative motivation ("I shouldn't do this or that").

a. If a Christian truly understands his union with Christ and sincerely desires to seek the things above, he will naturally put off those things that aren't pleasing to Christ (Colossians 3:5–9). What else should he do (Colossians 3:10)?

_____

b. The spiritual "replacement principle" (putting off and putting on) is an important spiritual concept. The phrase **put on the new man** cannot refer to salvation because it would make man the author of his own redemption. What do you think this phrase means (Colossians 3:10)?

_____

_____

_____

_____

_____

8. The spiritual rebirth that Christ offers mankind has profound implications. Man, once enslaved to sin and mired in an earthly existence without meaning or hope, is rescued by the King of kings. The believer is given a new perspective on life (Colossians 3:1–4), a new power over sin (Colossians 3:5–9), and a new priority—to love others (Colossians 3:10–4:2). What else happens when a child of God is **renewed in knowledge according to the image of Him who created him** (Colossians 3:10–11; Galatians 3:28)?

_____

_____

_____

_____

_____

_____

_____

EIGHT

BECOMING GOD'S MAN

Read Colossians 3:12–25; other references as given.

In the previous lesson you learned that Christ's supremacy over all things includes the believer's thoughts and actions. The Christian should put off the sinful habits of the old (unsaved) life, because he has (spiritually) died with Christ (Colossians 3:3).

In Colossians 3:12–25 you'll learn how a believer responds to life in a fallen world. No longer enslaved to the sins of the flesh, he allows Christ to live through him for the glory of God. You'll also learn that Christ's supremacy extends over your general attitudes and actions (Colossians 3:12–17), marriage and family relationships (Colossians 3:18–21), and your work life (Colossians 3:22–25). The detailed instruction in this passage emphasizes Christ's preeminence over every aspect of our lives.

Now ask God to reveal Himself to you through His Word and to transform you into the image of Jesus Christ.

1. Paul instructs the Colossian believers to adopt certain Christian virtues that reflect their new nature as **the elect of God, holy and beloved** (Colossians 3:12). Living in harmony with God's plan is a powerful witness of Christ's power to change lives (John 13:34–35; 17:21–23).

   a. God expects His diverse family (Colossians 3:11) to live in harmony with one another. To accomplish this, Christians must clothe themselves with **tender mercies, kindness, humbleness of mind, meekness,** [and]

Many groups study the Final Exam the week after the final lesson for three reasons: (1) someone might come to Christ, (2) believers gain assurance of salvation, (3) group members learn how to share the gospel.

———

ADD GROUP
INSIGHTS BELOW

longsuffering (Colossians 3:12). Mercy (Gk. *oiktirmon*) is a Christian virtue that causes a believer to be moved with feelings of tenderness while he or she attempts to relieve the sufferings and needs of others. In what ways do the sufferings and needs of others consistently cause you to help relieve their distress?

_____

_____

_____

b. **Kindness** (Gk. *chrestotes*) combines the qualities of goodness, gentleness, and graciousness. It might be defined as "sweetness of disposition." Does this describe your general disposition as you conduct the routine affairs of life

1. ... in your home?
    Yes / No / Not as much as it should
2. ... at work?
    Yes / No / Not as much as it should
3. ... with other Christians?
    Yes / No / Not as much as it should
4. ... among non-Christians
    Yes / No / Not as much as it should

c. **Humility** (Greek: *tapeinophrosne*) and **meekness** (Greek: *prautes*) are spiritual characteristics essential for harmonious relations with others. **Longsuffering** (Greek: *makrothumia*) denotes the self-restraint that enables a believer to bear insult or injury without resorting to retaliation. What could you do to manifest these three qualities more fully when you feel threatened or attacked at work, at home, or at church?

_____

_____

_____

2. a. The phrase **bearing with one another** defines the believer's goal of putting up with the minor irritations and the imperfections of others. Are you more or less willing to bear with the faults of others than you were a year ago? Give an example if you can.

    _____

    _____

    _____

    b. How does **bearing with one another** differ from quietly resenting another person?

    _____

    _____

    _____

    _____

3. Even though God's people can be very diligent about incorporating these qualities into their lives, they will still fall short of fulfilling His plan if they don't let love motivate their actions (Colossians 3:14; 1 Corinthians 13:1). Besides love, what else should a Christian do to fulfill God's plan for his life (Colossians 3:15–17)?

    _____

    _____

    _____

    _____

    _____

    _____

4. Many Christians understand their relationship with God to be purely vertical. While concentrating on their heavenly relationship with Christ, they forget that He has placed them into the family of God on earth. List the phrases that

If the leader asks all the study questions, the group discussion will be more likely to stay on track.

ADDITIONAL INSIGHTS

ADDITIONAL
INSIGHTS

specifically identify the believer's responsibility to other members of the body of Christ (Colossians 3:9–17; for example: **do not lie to one another** [Colossians 3:9]).

_____

_____

_____

_____

_____

_____

5. a. Beginning in Colossians 3:18 the Bible addresses how Christ's supremacy applies to marriage and family relations. How does a married Christian woman acknowledge Christ's supremacy in her life (Colossians 3:18)?

_____

_____

   b. How can a married Christian man and father acknowledge Christ's supremacy in his life (Colossians 3:19, 21)?

_____

_____

_____

   c. How can children acknowledge Christ's supremacy in their lives (Colossians 3:20)?

_____

6. Some Christians reject the biblical teaching of the man's leadership and female's submission to his leadership within the marriage bond. They believe that Christ's death eliminated all social and gender distinctions (Galatians 3:28) and that the biblical passages that promote the wife's

submission are culturally obsolete. While Christ's death does provide every person equal access to God, it doesn't remove the male leadership within the marriage bond.

a. List two reasons why the biblical teaching regarding the wife's submission to her husband should not be ignored.

1. _____

_____ (Colossians 3:18)

2. _____

_____ (1 Corinthians 11:12)

b. List at least three truths taught in Colossians 3:18 about the wife's submission in marriage.

1. _____

_____ .

2. _____

_____ .

3. _____

_____ .

7. Having completed his instruction on the family, Paul now addresses the relationship between the servant and his master (Colossians 3:22–4:1). The servant of Paul's day was to demonstrate his willingness to acknowledge the supremacy of Christ by submitting to his master (Colossians 3:22). How can a Christian worker demonstrate that he or she acknowledges Christ's supremacy (Colossians 3:22–24)?

1. _____

_____

_____ (v. ____)

2. _____

It's time to order your next study. Allow enough time to get the books so you can distribute them at the Open House. Consider ordering 2-3 extra books for newcomers.

ADDITIONAL INSIGHTS

_____

_____ (v. _____)

3. _____

_____

_____ (v. _____)

4. _____

_____

_____ (v. _____)

5. _____

_____

_____ (v. _____)

8. a. If you are a Christian, do your workplace performance, attitudes, and conduct and your family life (including your marriage) reveal Christ's preeminence in your life?

_____

b. If not, what changes could you make immediately (today—remember the word *now* in Colossians 3:8) that would demonstrate that you love Jesus Christ and acknowledge His supremacy over every aspect of your life?

_____

_____

_____

_____

NINE

WITNESSES OF CHRIST'S SUPREMACY

Read Colossians 4; other references as given.

In the previous two lessons you learned that Christ's supremacy is not just a sterile theological truth. It has profound implications for every believer. Jesus' preeminence extends from the highest realms of the universe (the heavens, the angelic world; Colossians 1:16) to the depths of the human heart (Colossians 3;12,15). All things were created by Him and for Him. And it is by His will and power that all things hold together (Colossians 1:17).

In this last lesson it's easy to read the apostle Paul's final words to the Colossians as merely a collection of personal greetings to fellow Christian workers and friends. But they are much more than that. His final words are the divinely inspired record of ordinary people who did extraordinary things because they surrendered their lives to God and let Christ live through them. Their lives may appear distant because of the years, but they fulfill these words in Hebrews, **we also, since we are surrounded by so great a cloud of witnesses** (Hebrews 12:1). As you complete this final lesson, let their lives inspire you to live wholeheartedly for Jesus Christ.

Now ask God to reveal Himself to you through His Word and to transform you into the image of Jesus Christ.

1. The Bible is the inspired Word of God, but the chapter and verse divisions were added much later. In AD 1227, University of Paris professor Stephen Langton (Langton later became

Final Exam:

Are you meeting next week to study the Final Exam? To learn how to present it effectively, contact Lamplighters.

———

ADD GROUP INSIGHTS BELOW

the Archbishop of Canterbury) added the chapter divisions. Langton's chapter divisions were adopted by John Wycliffe, whose Bible in English was the first divided throughout into chapters, and nearly all translations follow his chapter divisions.

a. Colossians 4:1 is a conclusion of Paul's instruction to the Colossian believers regarding employees' responsibilities to their employers and employers' responsibilities to their workers (Colossians 3:22–4:1). How can a Christian employer reflect his or her acknowledgment of Christ's authority over his life and work (Colossians 4:1)?

_____

_____

_____

b. The biblical instruction of Christian leadership not only includes just and fair compensation for all employees but also addresses leadership style and methodology. What must every Christian employer refrain from doing to his or her employees (Ephesians 6:9)? Why?

_____

_____

_____

2. The command to **continue earnestly in prayer, being vigilant in it with thanksgiving** (Colossians 4:2) could apply directly to both employers and employees, but the command has a broader application to all believers, regardless of their work. This verse teaches several important truths about effective prayer. List at least three.

1. _____

   _____

2. _____

Would you like to learn how to lead someone through this same study? It's not hard. Go to www.Lamplighters USA.org to register for *free* online leadership training.

ADDITIONAL INSIGHTS

3. _____

3. On several occasions Paul asked the churches to pray for him (Ephesians 6:19; 1 Thessalonians 5:25; 2 Thessalonians 3:1). What did Paul ask the Colossian believers to pray for on his behalf (Colossians 4:3–4)?

_____

_____

_____

4. What do you think it means to **walk in wisdom toward those who are outside** (Colossians 4:5)?

_____

_____

_____

5. Many scholars believe that the original concerns about the ministry and the Colossian heresies were brought to Paul by Epaphras (Colossians 1:7–8). Paul's letter to the Colossians was subsequently hand delivered by Tychicus and Onesimus (Colossians 4:7–9). How does Paul describe these two Christian servants?

_____

_____

6. At the time of Paul's letter to the Colossians it appears that Epaphras was not planning to return to the church. Apparently the spiritual oversight of the church had been assumed by Archippus (Colossians 4:17).

a. How did Epaphras continue to minister to the believers at Colossae and the other churches of the Lycus Valley

(Laodicea, Hierapolis) after his departure (Colossians 4:12–13)?

_____

_____

_____

b. Paul's letter was originally sent to the saints and faithful brethren at Colossae (Colossians 1:2). What did Paul want Tychicus and Onesimus to tell Archippus (Colossians 4:17)? What do you think this means?

_____

_____

7. Paul's final request for the Colossian believers was that God's grace might be extended to them (Colossians 4:18). Like many of Paul's letters to the churches, the book of Colossians begins with grace (**Grace to you and peace from God our Father and the Lord Jesus Christ**; Colossians 1:2) and ends with grace (**Grace be with you**; Colossians 4:18).

a. These statements (**Grace to you, Grace be with you**) are more than ancient customary greetings and standard closings. God's grace is the key that opens His vault of forgiveness for eternal life, and it is the sustaining power to live victoriously for Christ. Give a biblical definition of God's grace in one complete sentence. Try to refrain from using some tidy definition or acronym you may have heard in the past.

_____

_____

_____

b. Grace is something undeserved; something God extends to unwarranted sinners who have violated His holiness. What does the Bible teach about grace in relationship to man's salvation (Ephesians 2:8–9)?

_____

_____

8. Summarize the central theme or message of the book of Colossians in one complete sentence.

_____

_____

_____

9. What were the three most significant spiritual truths you learned from this study of the book of Colossians?

1. _____

_____

2. _____

_____

3. _____

_____

• • • •

Congratulations:

You have just completed a challenging study of a very special book of the Bible. If you have completed all nine lessons, you will likely have a better understanding of Christ's supremacy and how this profound truth should affect your life. You must reject the emptiness of worldly philosophies, the bondage of legalism, the subjectivity and confusion of mysticism, and the misplaced confidence of asceticism. Seek those things which are above, where Christ sits at the right hand of God (Colossians 3:1), knowing that of the Lord you will receive the reward of the inheritance (Colossians 3:24). Grace be with you (Colossians 4:18).

LEADER'S GUIDE

Lesson 1: The Life-Changing Gospel

1. Saints and faithful brethren (brothers) in Christ.

2. 1. Children of God (John 1:12). 2. Sons (Galatians 4:5). 3. Heirs (Galatians 4:7). 4. A chosen generation (1 Peter 2:9). 5. A royal priesthood (1 Peter 2:9). 6. A holy nation (1 Peter 2:9). 7. A special people (1 Peter 2:9).

3. a. He was thankful for their faith in Christ and their love for other Christians.
    b. 1. He prayed for them regularly (Colossians 1:3).
        2. He told them he was grateful for the letter.
    c. Answers will vary.

4. a. 1. All the world (Colossians 1:6). 2. All wisdom (Colossians 1:9). 3. All might (Colossians 1:11). 4. All patience and longsuffering (Colossians 1:11). 5. All creation (Colossians 1:15). 6. All things (Colossians 1:16–18, five times). 7. All fullness (Colossians 1:19). 8. All things (Colossians 1:20). 9. All wisdom (Colossians 1:28).
    b. The remarkable frequency of the word *all* emphasizes the universality of the plan of God in this world. It refutes the Colossian errorists' claim of secret, special enlightenment that trapped their naive followers into an addictive spiritual bondage. There is a powerful spiritual lesson for believers of all ages—God's truth is universal, and He gives spiritual understanding to all who come to Him in faith.

5. Hope is viewed as a treasure that is being accumulated in heaven. This hope is credited to a specific account (**for you**) and the place of that deposit is **heaven**. Interestingly, a clear perspective of eternity (the believer's hope) affects our attitude toward present circumstances. In Scripture hope is not an uncertain belief in a future event (as in "I hope this happens") but a settled reality yet to be realized. There is no uncertainty regarding future fulfillment. Thus the future can be said to determine the present, for what is reserved in heaven for the believer now exercises a decisive influence upon his present conduct.

6. a. The word of the truth which is the gospel (Colossians 1:5).

   b. The Greek construction of this phrase reveals that the Word of God goes forth in and of itself bearing fruit. This means that while it is incumbent upon Christians to spread the Good News because of the command of the Lord Jesus (Matthew 28:18–20; Mark 16:15), the gospel also goes forth throughout the world to reach the lost. Believers should spread the message of Christ's salvation to the lost, but they must also realize that a person's salvation is the result of a sovereign God's work in and on behalf of the sinner.

7. a. As a dear fellow servant and a faithful minister of Christ.

   b. Answers will vary.

8. He prayed that they would be filled with the knowledge of God's will in all spiritual wisdom and understanding.

9. 1. They should bear fruit in everything they do (Colossians 1:10).

   2. They should learn God's Word (Colossians 1:10).

   3. They should allow God's grace to strengthen them for every spiritual task (Colossians 1:11).

   4. They should conduct their various duties in life with an attitude of grateful praise to God the Father (Colossians 1:12).

Lesson 2: The Supremacy of Christ

1. a. 1. It is God who delivers man from the power of darkness. Man does not rescue himself.

      2. God's deliverance is a finished act: "He delivered us."

      3. Man can experience the assurance of this deliverance. Paul spoke with assurance of his personal deliverance.

      4. Man is either living in the domain of darkness or in the kingdom of Jesus Christ. There is no other option or place.

      5. Other answers could apply.

   b. 1. A new creation (2 Corinthians 5:17).

      2. An ambassador (2 Corinthians 5:20).

      3. A citizen of heaven (Philippians 3:20).

2. a. The Greek word for image (*eikon*, cf. icon — image) expresses two ideas. Christ is the likeness or image of God the Father in the sense that He is the exact likeness of Him, like the reflection of one in a mirror (Hebrews 1:3). The second idea in the word is manifestation. Jesus Christ is the image of God the Father in the sense that He reveals the nature and being of God (John 1:18). Paul's statement leaves no room for the Colossian heretic's vague concept of the partial deity who was becoming progressively more and more God (modern-day Mormonism, New Age, etc.).

 b. Both. The primary meaning appears to be first in rank. The term *firstborn* does not refer to temporary priority but to Christ's unique supremacy over all creation. As all things were created through Him and for Him (Colossians 1:16), He stands over His creation as both Lord and Master.

3. a. 1. All things were created by Him (Colossians 1:16).
   2. All things were created for Him (Colossians 1:16).
   3. In Him all things consist (Colossians 1:17).

 b. Answers will vary.

4. Christ is both the unifying principle and the personal sustainer of all creation. The unity of the creation derives its cohesiveness and continuance from its Creator, Jesus Christ. He is, as one scholar said, "the principle of cohesion" who makes the universe "a cosmos instead of a chaos."

5. a. In a local church every aspect of the ministry should acknowledge the supremacy of Christ and willingly submit to His headship and authority. There should be a repudiation of all attempts to build a kingdom of man that brings glory to men but fails to acknowledge the will of God and the authority of His Word. The effectiveness of church ministries should not be evaluated by human standards, but by their adherence to the lordship of Christ. This does not mean that new methods of ministry should not be tried. They are acceptable as long as they adhere to the principles of God's Word.

 b. 1. Using worldly methods that pander to the fleshly appetites and felt-needs of the people but compromise the clear preaching and teaching of God's Word.
   2. Using secular psychology in counseling that contradicts the plain

teaching of God's Word.

3. Focusing on numerical growth of the church rather than faithfulness to God's Word as the standard of ministerial success.

4. Placing financial advancement of the church above spiritual influence as the criterion and evidence of God's blessing.

5. Other answers could apply.

6. It was God the Father's pleasure and will for all the sum and substance of divine entitlement to dwell in Christ. Christ was not partially God or becoming God. He always was and always will be the very embodiment of all that was and ever will be God. The great biblical scholar John Calvin understood the word *fullness* (Gk. *pleroma*) to mean "fullness of righteousness, wisdom, power, and every blessing," explaining that "whatever God has, He has conferred upon His Son." This statement confronted the Colossian heretic's idea that supernatural beings (Christ included) were in the process of becoming God. The word *dwell* (Gk. *katoikeo*) emphasizes the permanent residence of the fullness of Christ's deity.

7. a. Man is delivered from the domain of darkness and transferred to the kingdom of Jesus Christ by a sovereign act of a loving God who died on a cross (Colossians 1:13, 20). Christ's death on the cross removed the enmity between God and man (God's wrath; John 3:36) and brings peace (the absence of hostility) to all those who exercise sincere faith in Christ's redemptive act (Colossians 1:23). Those who trust in Christ alone for eternal life are reconciled to God and are holy and blameless and beyond reproach in His sight (positional sanctification).

b. Answers will vary.

Lesson 3: Standing with Christ

1. 1. He willingly suffered for the cause of Christ.

2. He maintained a Christ-honoring attitude (rejoiced) in the face of adversity.

2. a. 1. Paul understood and accepted the doctrine of God's sovereignty (Colossians 1:16). This allowed him to accept personal trials and

difficulties as part of God's providential plan for his life to bring glory to Him.

2. Paul accepted God's authority over all aspects of his life including his attitude (Colossians 1:18, **that in all things he may have the preeminence**). Because Paul saw his present situation (imprisonment) as a part of God's plan, he was able to accept it as an opportunity for spiritual service rather than as human misfortune.

b. Answers will vary.

3. 1. He wrote letters of instruction and encouragement to the other believers (Colossians 1:1–3).

2. He prayed for other believers (Colossians 1:9).

3. He praised God in the midst of difficult circumstances (Acts 16:25).

4. He witnessed to others of the saving power of Jesus Christ (Acts 16:28–32).

5. He continued to study the Word of God (2 Timothy 4:13).

4. a. 1. The book of Colossians teaches that Jesus has forgiven us of all our transgressions (Colossians 2:12–13).

2. The gospel of John teaches that the work of redemption is finished (John 19:30).

3. The book of Hebrews teaches that Jesus offered one sacrifice for sins for all time (Hebrews 10:10–12).

b. The Greek word for afflictions (*thlipsis*) is never used in the New Testament for Christ's sufferings on the cross. The word means "distress, pressure or trouble," which Paul experienced in generous supply (2 Corinthians 11:23–29). The Bible is teaching that Christ's relationship with His church is so intimate (Christ is the head and we are the body) that He continues to suffer vicariously when His followers are persecuted. Christ asked Saul on the road to Damascus, "Why do you persecute me?" (Acts 26:14)—an obvious reference to His vicarious suffering through the church, since He was in heaven. Paul was saying that he was willing to do his part for the work of Christ.

5. a. Stewardship (NIV: "commission") from God.

b. Answers will vary. Answers will vary. Answers will vary.

6. The mystery is not that a redeemer or messiah would come because that was promised throughout the Old Testament (Isaiah 9:6–7; Micah 5:2). Nor was the mystery that the Gentiles would be included in God's plan, for that also was prophesied (Isaiah 42:6, 49:6). The mystery was the true identity of the redeemer (Jesus Christ) and the timing of His revelation (**the fullness of the time**; Galatians 4:4). Even Paul himself did not fully understand the true identity of Jesus Christ when He revealed Himself to him on the road to Damascus. In Scripture a mystery is not something that is unknowable. It is a something that was previously unknown but has been revealed.

7. a. Paul and the other missionaries wanted to warn every person about the dangers of false teaching and teach everyone in wisdom. Their goal was to help every person become spiritually mature in Jesus Christ.

   b. Paul and his missionary companions labored and worked hard according to the power of God within them to accomplish their goal of helping others become mature in Christ.

   c. Answers will vary.

8. Answers will vary.

Lesson 4: Walking in Christ

1. The struggle or conflict was likely Paul's diligent prayer on behalf of those he had not met and about whom likely had only received scant information as to their spiritual well-being.

2. 1. He wanted their hearts to be knit together in love.
   2. He wanted them to come to a point of spiritual maturity.
   3. He wanted them to experience the full assurance of the knowledge of Christ.

3. 1. Christians learn to love one another, and their hearts are knit together in close fellowship. If a Christian does not participate in regular fellowship with other believers, he will not experience their love, which will help him grow in his faith in Christ. The spiritual encouragement that a Christian experiences from other believers is not only a source of comfort but is also the seedbed of spiritual growth.

2. Christians grow spiritually as they edify and encourage one another.

3. Christians gain assurance and confidence in the Lord when they are in close fellowship with one another.

4. Christians understand the mystery of God, namely that Jesus Christ is the promised Messiah—the One who was promised long ago and revealed in these last days.

4. a. Jesus Christ. In Him are hidden all the treasures of wisdom and knowledge. Jesus Christ has revealed Himself through His Word (John 17:17).

   b. 1. God's Word says we should worship God and no one and nothing else (Matthew 4:10).

     2. God's Word commands us not to worship idols because they do not (and cannot) reflect the true and complete character of God (Acts 17:29).

     3. When people worship anything other than God, it shows that they are missing the main thing, which is the true worship of God. To worship an image that was carved from something God made is to focus on the wrong thing. Relics, images, icons, idols, shrines, etc., draw genuine worshippers away from the true God. Worshipping idols is evidence of man's folly (Romans 1:22–23).

5. 1. Man (Romans 1:25)

   2. Self, important people, government leaders/heads of state (Acts 12:21–23).

   3. Shrines/Idols (Acts 19:26). Mythical figures (Diana; Acts 19:27).

6. a. 1. "I (Jesus) am the way, the truth, and the life" (John 14:6).

     2. "Sanctify them in the truth. Your Word is truth" (John 17:17).

   b. Answers will vary.

7. a. 1. The word *as* indicates a comparison. Individuals come to Christ in total humility and complete faith in Jesus' ability to save them, and they should continue to live their Christian lives in humble submission to Him and faith in Him.

     2. The word *walk* indicates the Christian life is not a serial fulfillment of daily Christian duties but a manner of living in which the believer communes with God as he or she conducts the affairs of everyday life.

b. The phrase **walk in Him** indicates a "spiritual togetherness with Jesus"—a willingness by the believer to keep spiritual pace with the calling of Jesus Christ and the leading of the Holy Spirit. Jesus told His disciples that He would abide in them and they were to abide in Him (John 15:4–6). To walk in Him means the Christian has renounced the self-life (walking with self), has repudiated performance-based Christianity, and embraces the love of God. He walks together in Christ each day and experiences the abundant life Christ promised (John 10:10). This life is filled with joy, grace, and the power of being filled with the Holy Spirit. This should be the believer's normal Christian life.

8.

1. **Sit** (Ephesians 2:6)	refers to the believer's present and eternal standing before God as a result of Jesus' finished work on his or her behalf.
2. **Rest** (Hebrews 4:9–10)	refers to the peace a believer can possess if he or she learns to trust fully in God's promises.
3. **Walk** (Colossians 2:6)	refers to the Christian's need to live by faith after salvation and to be led by the Holy Spirit.
4. **Run** (Hebrews 12:1)	refers to the believer's need for passion, purpose, endurance, and single-mindedness in his or her devotion to Christ.
5. **Stand** (Ephesians 6:14)	refers to the believer's responsibility to remain loyal to Christ in times of adversity through the power of the Holy Spirit.

9. Answers will vary.

Lesson 5: Reject Worldly Philosophies

1. a. 1. They are according to the traditions of men (it is humanistic).
   2. They are according to the basic teachings of this world.
   3. They are not in accordance with the teachings of Christ.
   b. The Colossian believers needed to comprehend the danger of this threat (**Beware**; Colossians 2:8). They were also to realize that accepting this type of teaching would **cheat** their spiritual lives (literally, plunder;

Colossians 2:18) and rob them of the richness of Jesus Christ. They were to guard themselves against these false teachings because they sounded plausible, but they were contrary to the teachings of Christ.

2. 1. The ultimate goal in life is to be happy and to help others be happy as well.
   2. What doesn't kill you makes you better.
   3. You can be anything you want to be.
   4. Every woman has the right to choose what happens to her body.
   5. Money is the secret to success.
   6. All religions are basically the same.
   7. God is too good to send anyone to hell.
   8. The world is millions and millions of years old.
   9. All things work together for good.
   10. All religions lead to God. There are just different paths.
   11. Every person has a spark of the divine in him or her. It just has to be acknowledged and fanned to become a reality.
   12. I know God forgives me, but I have to learn to forgive myself.
   13. You have to learn to love yourself before you can love others.
   14. Other answers could apply.

3. 1. God exposes the world's wisdom as foolishness (1 Corinthians 1:20) — for example, predictions that the world is going to run out of fuel by such-and-such a year, etc.
   2. It is unable to bring an individual to the knowledge of God (1 Corinthians 1:21).
   3. It is inferior to the wisdom of God (1 Corinthians 1:25).

4. a. Solomon said it was vanity or emptiness (Ecclesiastes 2:2).
   b. Solomon said it too was vanity, like grasping for the wind (Ecclesiastes 2:11). He also said it was not beneficial as long as he was living (Ecclesiastes 2:11).
   c. Solomon said gaining earthly wisdom is better than folly, but in the end they are both empty (Ecclesiastes 2:15).
   d. The whole purpose of living is to fear God and obey or keep His commandments (Ecclesiastes 12:13). God will judge everyone, and their secrets will be brought into judgment (Ecclesiastes 12:14). Answers will vary.

5. God's thoughts are different than man's thoughts. God's ways and His thoughts are higher (better, based upon a higher wisdom) than man's thoughts.

6. a. He allowed his thoughts to be confronted with the truth of God's Word. When his thoughts contradicted the Word of God, he deliberately chose to relinquish his own ideas and accept the teachings of the Word of God. Paul regarded his own thoughts as enemies if they conflicted with the Word of God. He zealously eliminated all thoughts from his mind that were opposed to the truth (**every high thing, every thought**).
   b. Answers will vary.
   c. Answers will vary.

7. There is likely not a more powerful verse in the Bible for the true believer to comprehend. Paul already told the Colossians that in Christ all the fullness of the Godhead dwells in bodily form (Colossians 2:9), and he follows that up with the statement that Christians, because of their inseparable union with Christ, are complete. Everything Christ provides in salvation belongs to the believer, and everything Christ promises as a result of salvation is available to the believer on the basis of acceptance by faith. This includes peace with God (Romans 5:1–2), freedom from a sinful past (2 Corinthians 5:17), an abundant life filled with meaning and purpose (1 Corinthians 10:31; 2 Corinthians 5:18–20) victory over sin (1 Corinthians 10:13), wisdom (James 1:5), the fruit of the Spirit (Galatians 5:22–23), plus much more. No wonder the Bible says, **You are complete in Him**.

8. a. 1. The Christian must present his or her body (entire being) as a living sacrifice (Romans 12:1).
      2. The Christian must not allow the worldly enticements of this world to become his focus or passionate pursuit (Romans 12:2).
      3. The Christian must allow his or her mind to be transformed by God's Word (Romans 12:2).
   b. Paul viewed himself as having died with Christ (been **crucified**), and he viewed his new life in Christ as an entirely new life that was to be lived by faith in God. To Paul, this seemed like a reasonable thing to do, since Christ loved Him and had died for him (Galatians 2:20). Paul saw himself as a prisoner of Jesus Christ—One who had arrested him

by His life and grace and One he would gladly serve the rest of his life (Ephesians 3:1).

Lesson 6: Dangerous Detours

1. 1. Romans says that believers are not under the law, but under grace (Romans 6:14).
   2. Christ is the end of the law for righteousness to everyone who believes (Romans 10:4).
   3. The book of Galatians says that the Old Testament law was our tutor to bring us to Christ (Galatians 3:19–25). When a person comes to Christ in salvation, he or she is no longer under the Law (the tutor, guardian, schoolmaster).

2. a. 1. Religious standards for personal dress (clothing, makeup, style and length of hair, etc.) that are not supported by Scripture.
      2. Religious standards that require adherents to eat or refrain from certain foods (Romans 14:1–3).
      3. Religious standards related to specific "holy days" that are identified in Scripture (Romans 14:5–6).
      4. Any religious teaching that goes beyond what the Bible teaches and that holds others (followers) to a standard or commitment that is not supported by God's Word.
   b. Answers will vary. Reject them.

3. a. Paul said the Colossian Christians had been circumcised (not the human kind) with the "spiritual circumcision" by Christ at salvation (Colossians 2:11, **made without hands**). Spiritual circumcision removes the believer's sins and the guilt related to them.
   b. Salvation.

4. a. Christ removed the penalty of our sin and raised us up with Him through faith (in his finished work on our behalf; Colossians 2:11–12). He forgave all our trespasses (past, present, and future) and made us alive together with Him (Colossians 2:13), and totally removed the list (handwriting of requirements) of the legal requirements of the Law that indicted us and made us guilty as charged on all counts. All charges against us were dropped because Jesus Christ Himself took them

away and nailed them to the cross so we could never be charged with them again (Colossians 2:14–15).

b. Answers will vary.

5. a. 1. Mysticism often leads to spiritual pride (**vainly puffed up by his fleshly mind**; Colossians 2:18).

   2. Mysticism often draws people away from God (**not holding fast to the Head** [Christ]; Colossians 2:19).

   b. 1. Allegorizing or spiritualizing God's Word, which is assigning a "spiritual" meaning to a Bible verse or passage—one that is speculative and is not supported by Scripture.

   2. Emphasis on spiritual impressions ("God spoke to me to say this or that").

   3. Endeavoring to determine God's will by "fleece-casting," whereby the believer attempts to discern God's direction for his or her life by assigning an arbitrary meaning to an external event or a subjective impression rather than looking to God's Word. The term "fleece-casting" comes from Judges 6:36–40, where Gideon asked God twice for signs to confirm what He had already commanded Gideon to do. God's willingness to reveal the signs to Gideon should not be construed as His endorsement, nor should it become a model for Christian decision-making.

6. a. Asceticism appears to be a legitimate method of attempting to control the desires of the sin nature because the ascetic is endeavoring to restrict the fulfillment of its appetites—the perceived source of man's sin problem. The problem, however, is that the flesh (man's sin nature) does not have the power to overcome its own fallenness. One Christian put it this way: "You can't control the flesh with the flesh. It's too weak." To overcome the sinful nature of man requires spiritual transformation, not personal reformation, and that only comes through faith in Jesus Christ.

   b. Asceticism has no strength or ability to overcome the desires or appetites (**indulgence**) of the flesh or the sinful nature of man.

7. a. Answers will vary.

   b. The Christian should be encouraged to look to the Word of God and realize that he or she is complete in Christ. When we add worldly philosophies, legalism, mysticism, or asceticism to our spiritual lives, we are not strengthening them; we are weakening the effect that Christ could have and wants to have in our lives.

Lesson 7: From Rags to Riches

1. a. He should be constantly seeking the things of God.
    b. The believer should center his or her spiritual attention on Christ. All thoughts and attitudes, actions, and life goals should reflect Christ's supremacy. The believer's devotion to Christ should take precedence over all earthly allegiances.

2. The Christian is commanded to keep seeking the things of Christ (Colossians 3:1). The Greek verb *zeteo* means to seek, desire, or strive after by thinking, meditating, or reasoning. The word means a constant searching (present-tense command) for those interests that center in Christ. The second command (Gk. *phroneo*—to set your mind on something, to savor) refers more to a settled inner disposition. While the first command focuses more on the practical and deliberate choices that a believer makes in life, the second refers to the inner conviction that Christ is the only object worthy of the believer's continuing devotion. As one commentator said, "You must not only seek heaven, you must also think heaven."

3. The believer must consider how the affairs of his daily life can reflect his acknowledgement of Christ's authority. The Christian should not live for pleasure or self-advancement (the way of the world), nor should he or she view life as a dichotomy of the spiritual and the secular. The believer must see his vocation as a calling and a commission from God in which he is to glorify God in all he does. When a believer adopts this perspective, he will see the physical administration of the affairs of life from an eternal point of view. The Christian becomes less frustrated with the minor irritations of living in a fallen world and turns potential frustrations into opportunities to be a powerful witness for Christ.

4. a. Fornication, uncleanness, passion, evil desire, and covetousness.
    b. Answers will vary.
    c. Idolatry. Answers will vary

5. a. Now.
    b. 1. Anger. 2. Wrath. 3. Malice. 4. Blasphemy. 5. Filthy language. 6. Lying.

6. a. Jesus told the woman to **go and sin no more** (John 8:11). When a person is saved, the individual is indwelt with the very presence of God in the person of the Holy Spirit. The individual is freed from the penalty of sin (the wrath of God) and the power of sin. This does not mean that the person will live a sinless life (1 John 1:10), but it means the person possesses the power not to sin. The reason we sin after we are saved is because we are not trusting completely in God at that moment.
    b. 1. A Christian will never face a temptation but that God will supply the power for him or her to overcome that temptation through Christ (1 Corinthians 10:13).
        2. Christ came to destroy (render powerless) the works of the devil. The works of the devil are to get all people to doubt God and tempt them to turn away from God (1 John 3:8).

7. a. The Christian must **put on the new man** (Colossians 3:10).
    b. Putting on the new man refers to the spiritual transformation that happens when the believer is allowing his mind to be renewed by God and His Word and bringing his thoughts and actions into line with His will. This does not mean that the Christian can do this as a simple act of self-determination (Hebrews 6:1–3). He must learn to walk in the Spirit and trust God to give him the power to obey Christ's commands. On the other hand, God expects believers to take personal responsibility to live by faith and become all He wants them to be.

8. The phrase **have put on the new man** refers to the new nature that Christ gave the believer at the time of salvation (cf. 2 Corinthians 5:17 KJV; **a new creature**). However, the completion of the sanctification process in the life of the believer is a result of the continuing work of God and the continual submission of the believer. (Note: the Greek word for "have put on" is a middle participle.) The constant renewal of the new nature (cf. Colossians 3:10 KJV; **which is renewed**) allows the Christian to put off the practices of the old sinful nature and come to a true knowledge or understanding of Christ.

Lesson 8: Becoming God's Man

1. a. Answers will vary.
   b. Answers will vary.
   c. Answers will vary.

2. a. Answers will vary.
   b. When a Christian bears with the character imperfections of another person, he or she doesn't allow the person's weaknesses or failures to trouble them emotionally or spiritually. The believer understands the fallenness of all men, including himself, and celebrates God's grace rather than focusing on the person's failures. The Christian truly "bears" the failures of others. On the other hand, when a Christian resents another person's weaknesses or failures, he or she is demonstrating an unloving, judgmental spirit toward the other person.

3. 1. Believers should allow (God's) peace to rule in their hearts (Colossians 3:15).
   2. Believers should realize that they are part of one body—the universal body of Christ (Colossians 3:15). The phrase *one body* refers to all those who are genuinely born again throughout the world.
   3. Believers are to be thankful. Being thankful is more than adopting a positive mental attitude. When a Christian lives a life of thankfulness, it's an indication that he or she is trusting in God's sovereignty and sees each day as a gift from God and an opportunity to praise His name—an opportunity that he or she will never have again.
   4. Believers are to allow God's Word to **dwell richly** in their minds (preoccupy them; Colossians 3:16). One of the ways Christians can do this is to minister to one another with psalms, hymns, and spiritual songs and to meditate on the things of God in their hearts. These phrases speak to a Christian's preoccupation with the person and presence of God and learning to walk in the Spirit (Colossians 3:16).
   5. Believers see all life as spiritual rather than the common misconception of seeing life as both spiritual and secular. They are to do *everything* in the name of the Lord (Colossians 3:17), including responding with thankfulness for the trials and difficulties that their sovereign God allows to come into their lives.

4. 1. "Do not lie to one another" (Colossians 3:9).
   2. "Bearing with one another" (Colossians 3:13).
   3. "Forgiving one another" (Colossians 3:13).
   4. "Forgiving, if anyone has a complaint against another" (Colossians 3:13).
   5. "In all wisdom, teaching and admonishing one another" (Colossians 3:16).
   6. Other answers could include: "Put on tender mercies..." (Colossians 3:12).

5. a. She can be subject to her husband (Colossians 3:18).
   b. He can love his wife and not be harsh with her (Colossians 3:19). He should not cause his children to become bitter by overcorrecting them or living a hypocritical life before them (Colossians 3:21).
   c. They can be obedient to their parents.

6. a. 1. The command is stated clearly in Scripture (Colossians 3:18). It is a dangerous thing to simply eliminate a biblical command on cultural grounds. If this perspective is used without legitimate biblical basis, essentially every command in Scripture could be eliminated.
      2. The male headship of the family in some ways reflects the administrative order of the Godhead (1 Corinthians 11:12). The submission of the wife models the administrative subordination of Jesus Christ to God the Father. It is important to realize that, in both situations (husband–wife; God the Father–Jesus Christ the Son), subordination does not mean inferiority.
   b. 1. The wife's obedience is voluntary. It is never to be forced upon the wife by the husband.
      2. The wife's obedience is limited to her husband's authority as delegated by God. The Bible does not teach male superiority over women (chauvinism).
      3. The wife's obedience is restricted to the parameters of Scripture. She is not obligated to follow her husband if his demands directly conflict with specific spiritual commands (Acts 5:29). However, if she must defer to the authority of the Bible rather than obey her husband, she must continue to demonstrate an attitude of humility and respect. The biblical teaching emphasizes individual

responsibility within the marriage union rather than the rights of the individual partners. This does not mean that there are no implied rights within marriage. It does mean that each marriage partner should focus on their individual responsibilities rather than what their spouse is or is not doing within the marriage.

7. 1. Christian workers should work hard all the time, not just when they think they are being watched by their superiors (**not with eye service, as men-pleasers**; Colossians 3:22).

   2. Christian workers should do their work sincerely and perform admirably (**but in sincerity of heart**; Colossians 3:22).

   3. Christian workers should work to please God. They should realize that they are actually working to please God by their efforts and quality of work (**fearing God**; Colossians 3:22).

   4. Christian workers should give their best at work, including being conscientious about the smallest details of their work (**whatever you do, do it heartily, as to the Lord, and not to men**; Colossians 3:23). They should do their work as an act of worship to God and witness to others of His supremacy over their lives.

   5. Christian workers should realize that God is watching them and will eventually reward them for their efforts (Colossians 3:24).

   6. Christian workers should understand that God will not shield or deliver them from the consequences of a poor work performance (Colossians 3:25). If God's people do not fulfill their work responsibilities, they will reap the consequences of their error (termination, demotion, probation, etc.). They cannot expect God to supernaturally protect them if they are insubordinate or slothful (**there is no partiality**).

8. a. Answers will vary.
   b. Answers will vary.

Lesson 9: Witnesses of Christ's Supremacy

1. a. The Christian employer must constantly remind himself (herself) that he has another Authority to whom he must ultimately answer. If the Christian employer remembers this important truth, he will treat his or her employees with justice and fairness.

b. The Christian employer must give up threatening (Ephesians 6:9). He or she must not use fear as their "motivator of choice." This does not mean that the Christian employer cannot and should not warn an employee of the potential consequences of a poor work performance. It simply means that the Christian employer should not make fear his or her default motivator.

2. 1. The Greek word for "continue" means holding something with strength, not neglecting or letting it drop. The early Christians continued or *devoted* themselves (cf. Acts 2:42, same Greek word) to the apostles' teaching and to fellowship, to the breaking of bread and to prayer. Christians should not neglect prayer, both corporate and private.
    2. The phrase "being watchful to this end" means never neglecting or growing weary or careless. Believers should never allow prayer to become a careless ritual. They should be diligent in prayer to God for themselves and others (Ephesians 6:18).
    3. The third phrase, "with thanksgiving," means that as believers pray, they should express their appreciation for what God has done and their confidence in His wisdom and power to do what is best.

3. Paul asked the Colossians to join him in prayer so that God would providentially open a free opportunity for the ministry of the gospel. The mystery is the entire, blessed, gospel message of God's universal redemption which is made available through Jesus Christ's work on the cross. Paul desired to make this magnificent truth clear to all who would listen (Colossians 3:4).

4. Paul exhorted the Colossian Christians to exercise wisdom in their daily contact with non-Christians. This would help eliminate any hindrances and stumbling blocks to the gospel message and help the unsaved be more receptive to the truth. Paul saw the unsaved not as a threat (the way many Christians do) but as the prize—lost people for whom Christ died.

5. Paul said Tychicus was his beloved brother, a faithful minister, and a fellow servant of the Lord (Colossians 4:7). He said Onesimus was his faithful and beloved brother (Colossians 4:9).

6. a. 1. He labored in prayer for them so that they would come to spiritual

maturity (stand firm and fully assured in the will of God; Colossians 4:12).

2. He had a deep concern for the believers of the region (Colossians 4:13).

3. He sought spiritual help from the apostle Paul to correct the doctrinal problem that had developed in the church.

b. Paul wanted Archippus to pay close attention to the ministry God had given him (the church) so that he might fulfill the work God had given him.

7. a. Answers will vary.

b. It is by grace through faith that man is saved. It is totally apart from works.

8. The book of Colossians teaches the supremacy of Christ over all creation, including all men and all aspects of human existence. There is no such thing as secular life.

9. Answers will vary.

ADDITIONAL INSIGHTS

FINAL EXAM

Every person will eventually stand before God in judgment—the final exam. The Bible says, **And it is appointed for men to die once, but after this the judgment** (Hebrews 9:27).

May I ask you a question? *If you died today, do you know for certain you would go to heaven?* I did not ask if you're religious or a church member, nor did I ask if you've had some encounter with God—a meaningful spiritual experience. I didn't even ask if you believe in God or angels or if you're trying to live a good life. The question I *am* asking is this: *If you died today, do you know for certain you would go to heaven?*

When you die, you will stand alone before God in judgment. You'll either be saved for all eternity, or you will be separated from God for all eternity in what the Bible calls the lake of fire (Romans 14:12; Revelation 20:11–15). Tragically, many religious people who believe in God are not going to be accepted by Him when they die.

> **Many will say to Me in that day, "Lord, Lord, have we not prophesied in Your name, cast out demons in Your name, and done many wonders in Your name?" And then I will declare to them, "I never knew you; depart from Me, you who practice lawlessness!"** (Matthew 7:22–23)

God loves you and wants you to go to heaven (John 3:16; 2 Peter 3:9). If you are not sure where you'll spend eternity, you are not prepared to meet God. God wants you to know for certain that you will go to heaven.

> **Behold, now is the accepted time; behold, now is the day of salvation.** (2 Corinthians 6:2)

The words **behold** and **now** are repeated because God wants you to know that you can be saved today. You do not need to hear those terrible words, **Depart from Me ....** Isn't that great news?

Jesus himself said, **You must be born again** (John 3:7). These aren't the words of a pastor, a church, or a particular denomination. They're the words of Jesus Christ himself. You *must* be born again (saved from eternal damnation) before you die; otherwise, it will be too late when you die! You can know for certain today that God will accept you into heaven when you die.

These things I have written to you who believe in the name of the Son of God, that you may know that you have eternal life.

(1 John 5:13)

The phrase **you may know** means that you can know for certain before you die that you will go to heaven. To be born again, you must understand and accept four essential spiritual truths. These truths are right from the Bible, so you know you can trust them—they are not man-made religious traditions. Now, let's consider these four essential spiritual truths.

Essential Spiritual Truth

#1

The Bible teaches that you are a sinner and separated from God.

No one is righteous in God's eyes. To be righteous means to be totally without sin, not even a single act.

There is none righteous, no, not one;
There is none who understands;
There is none who seeks after God.
They have all turned aside;
They have together become unprofitable;
There is none who does good, no, not one.
(Romans 3:10–12)

...for all have sinned and fall short of the glory of God.
(Romans 3:23)

Look at the words God uses to show that all men are sinners—**none, not one, all turned aside, not one**. God is making a point: all of us are sinners. No one is good (perfectly without sin) in His sight. The reason is sin.

Have you ever lied, lusted, hated someone, stolen anything, or taken God's name in vain, even once? These are all sins.

Are you willing to admit to God that you are a sinner? If so, then tell Him right now you have sinned. You can say the words in your heart or aloud—it doesn't matter which—but be honest with God. Now check the box if you have just admitted you are a sinner.

☐ God, I admit I am a sinner in Your eyes.

Spiritual
Death

Eternal
Life

Now, let's look at the second essential spiritual truth.

Essential Spiritual Truth

#2

The Bible teaches that you cannot save yourself or earn your way to heaven.

Man's sin is a very serious problem in the eyes of God. Your sin separates you from God, both now and for all eternity—unless you are born again.

For the wages of sin is death.
(Romans 6:23)

And you He made alive, who were dead in trespasses and sins.
(Ephesians 2:1)

Wages are a payment a person earns by what he or she has done. Your sin has earned you the wages of death, which means separation from God. If you die never having been born again, you will be separated from God after death.

You cannot save yourself or purchase your entrance into heaven. The Bible says that man is **not redeemed with corruptible things, like silver or gold** (1 Peter 1:18). If you owned all the money in the world, you still could not buy your entrance into heaven. Neither can you buy your way into heaven with good works.

For by grace you have been saved through faith, and that not of yourselves; it is the gift of God, not of works, lest anyone should boast. (Ephesians 2:8–9)

The Bible says salvation is **not of yourselves**. It is **not of works, lest anyone should boast**. Salvation from eternal judgment cannot be earned by doing good works; it is a gift of God. There is nothing you can do to purchase your way into heaven because you are already unrighteous in God's eyes.

If you understand you cannot save yourself, then tell God right now that you are a sinner, separated from Him, and you cannot save yourself. Check the box below if you have just done that.

☐ God, I admit that I am separated from You because of my sin. I realize that I cannot save myself.

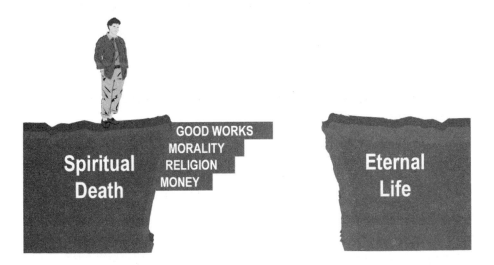

Now, let's look at the third essential spiritual truth.

Essential Spiritual Truth

#3

The Bible teaches that Jesus Christ died on the cross to pay the complete penalty for your sin and to purchase a place in heaven for you.

Jesus Christ, the sinless Son of God, lived a perfect life, died on the cross, and rose from the dead to pay the penalty for your sin and purchase a place in heaven for you. He died on the cross on your behalf, in your place, as your substitute, so you do not have to go to hell. Jesus Christ is the only acceptable substitute for your sin.

For He [God, the Father] made Him [Jesus] who knew [committed] no sin to be sin for us, that we might become the righteousness of God in Him.
(2 Corinthians 5:21)

I [Jesus] am the way, the truth, and the life. No one comes to the Father except through Me.
(John 14:6)

Nor is there salvation in any other, for there is no other name under heaven given among men by which we must be saved.
(Acts 4:12)

Jesus Christ is your only hope and means of salvation. Because you are a sinner, you cannot pay for your sins, but Jesus paid the penalty for your sins by dying on the cross in your place. Friend, there is salvation in no one else—not angels, not some religious leader, not even your religious good works. No religious act such as baptism, confirmation, or joining a church can save you. There is no other way, no other name that can save you. Only Jesus Christ can save you. You must be saved by accepting Jesus Christ's substitutionary sacrifice for your sins, or you will be lost forever.

Do you see clearly that Jesus Christ is the only way to God in heaven? If you understand this truth, tell God that you understand, and check the box below.

☐ God, I understand that Jesus Christ died to pay the penalty for my sin. I understand that His death on the cross was the only acceptable sacrifice for my sin.

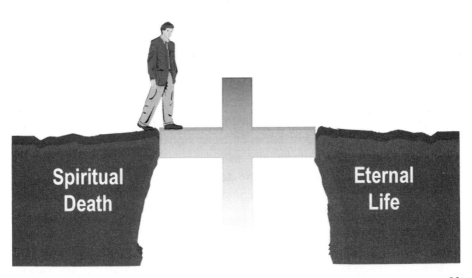

Spiritual Death

Eternal Life

Essential Spiritual Truth

#4

By faith, you must trust in Jesus Christ alone for eternal life and call upon Him to be your Savior and Lord.

Many religious people admit they have sinned. They believe Jesus Christ died for the sins of the world, but they are not saved. Why? Thousands of moral, religious people have never completely placed their faith in Jesus Christ *alone* for eternal life. They think they must believe in Jesus Christ as a real person and do good works to earn their way to heaven. They are not trusting Jesus Christ alone. To be saved, you must trust in Jesus Christ *alone* for eternal life. Look what the Bible teaches about trusting Jesus Christ alone for salvation.

Believe on the Lord Jesus Christ, and you will be saved.
(Acts 16:31)

...that if you confess with your mouth the Lord Jesus and believe in your heart that God has raised Him from the dead, you will be saved. For with the heart one believes unto righteousness, and with the mouth confession is made unto salvation.... For there is no distinction between Jew and Greek, for the same Lord over all is rich to all who call upon Him. For "whoever calls on the name of the Lord shall be saved.
(Romans 10:9–10, 12–13)

Do you see what God is saying? To be saved or born again, you must trust Jesus Christ *alone* for eternal life. Jesus Christ paid for your complete salvation. Jesus said, **It is finished!** (John 19:30). Jesus paid for your salvation completely when He shed His blood on the cross for your sin.

If you believe that God resurrected Jesus Christ (proving God's acceptance of Jesus as a worthy sacrifice for man's sin) and you are willing to confess Jesus Christ as your Savior and Lord (master of your life), you will be saved.

Friend, right now God is offering you the greatest gift in the world. God wants to give you the *gift* of eternal life, the *gift* of His complete forgiveness for all your sins, and the *gift* of His unconditional acceptance into heaven when you die. Will you accept His free gift now, right where you are?

Are you unsure how to receive the gift of eternal life? Let me help you. Do you remember that I said you needed to understand and accept four essential spiritual truths? First, you admitted you are a sinner. Second, you admitted you were separated from God because of your sin and you could not save yourself. Third, you realized that Jesus Christ is the only way to heaven—no other name can save you.

Now, you must trust that Jesus Christ died once and for all to save your lost soul. Just take God at His word—He will not lie to you! This is the kind of simple faith you need to be saved. If you would like to be saved right now, right where you are, offer this prayer of simple faith to God. Remember, the words must come from your heart.

> **God, I am a sinner and deserve to go to hell. Thank You, Jesus, for dying on the cross for me and for purchasing a place in heaven for me. I believe You are the Son of God and You are able to save me right now. Please forgive me for my sin and take me to heaven when I die. I invite You into my life as Savior and Lord, and I trust You alone for eternal life. Thank You for giving me the gift of eternal life. Amen.**

If, in the best way you know how, you trusted Jesus Christ alone to save you, then God just saved you. He said in His Holy Word, ***But as many as received Him, to them He gave the right to become the children of God***
(John 1:12). It's that simple. God just gave you the gift of eternal life by faith. You have just been born again, according to the Bible.

You will not come into eternal judgment, and you will not perish in the lake of fire—you are saved forever! Read this verse carefully and let it sink into your heart.

> *Most assuredly, I say to you, he who hears My word and believes in Him who sent Me has everlasting life, and shall not come into judgment, but has passed from death into life.*
> (John 5:24)

Now, let me ask you a few more questions.

According to God's holy Word (John 5:24), not your feelings, what kind of life did God just give you? _____

What two words did God say at the beginning of the verse to assure you that He is not lying to you? _____   _____

Are you going to come into eternal judgment? ❑ YES   ❑ NO

Have you passed from spiritual death into life? ❑ YES   ❑ NO

Friend, you've just been born again. You just became a child of God.

To help you grow in your new Christian life, we would like to send you some Bible study materials. To receive these helpful materials free of charge, e-mail your request to **info@LamplightersUSA.org.**

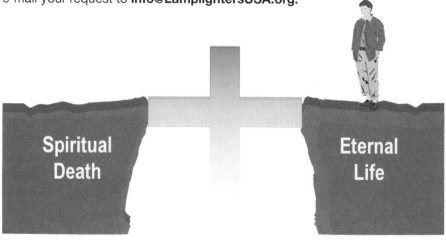

Spiritual
Death

Eternal
Life

Appendix

Level 1 (Basic Training)
Student Workbook

To begin, familiarize yourself with the Lamplighters' *Leadership Training and Development Process* (see graphic on page 98). Notice there are two circles: a smaller, inner circle and a larger, outer circle. The inner circle shows the sequence of weekly meetings beginning with an Open House, followed by an 8–14 week study, and concluding with a clear presentation of the gospel (Final Exam). The outer circle shows the sequence of the Intentional Discipleship training process (Leading Studies, Training Leaders, Multiplying Groups). As participants are transformed by God's Word, they're invited into a discipleship training process that equips them in every aspect of the intentional disciple-making ministry.

The Level 1 training (Basic Training) is *free*, and the training focuses on two key aspects of the training: 1) how to prepare a life-changing Bible study (ST-A-R-T) and 2) how to lead a life-changing Bible study (10 commandments). The training takes approximately 60 minutes to complete, and you complete it as an individual or collectively as a small group (preferred method) by inserting an extra week between the Final Exam and the Open House.

To begin your training, go to www.LamplightersUSA.org to register yourself or your group. A Lamplighters' Certified Trainer will guide you through the entire Level 1 training process. After you have completed the training, you can review as many times as you like.

When you have completed the Level 1 training, please consider completing the Level 2 (Advanced) training. Level 2 training will equip you to reach more people for Christ by learning how to train new leaders and by showing you how to multiply groups. You can register for additional training at www. LamplightersUSA.org.

Intentional Discipleship

Training & Development Process

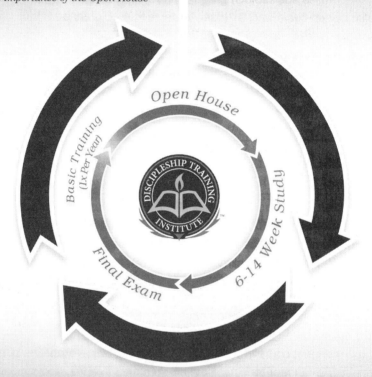

3. Multiplying Groups

The "5 Steps" for Starting New Groups

The Audio Training Library (ATL)

The Importance of the Open House

1. Leading Studies

ST-A-R-T

10 Commandments

Solving All Group Problems

Open House

Basic Training (1x Per Year)

6-14 Week Study

Final Exam

DISCIPLESHIP TRAINING INSTITUTE

2. Training Leaders

Four-fold ministry of a leader

The Three Diagnostic Questions

The 2P's for recruiting new leaders

The three stages of leadership training

How to Prepare a
Life-Changing Bible Study
ST-A-R-T

Step 1: _____ and _____.

Pray specifically for the group members and yourself as you study God's Word. Ask God (_____) to give each group member a rich time of personal Bible study, and thank (_____) God for giving you a desire to invest in the spiritual advancement of each other.

Step 2: _____ the _____.

Answer the questions in the weekly lessons without looking at the _____ _____.

Step 3: _____and _____.

Review the Leader's Guide, and _____ every truth you missed when you originally did your lesson. Record the answers you missed with a _____ _____ so you'll know what you missed.

Step 4: _____ _____.

Calculate the specific amount of time _____ _____ to spend on each question and write the start time next to each one in the _____ using a _____.

How to Lead a Life-Changing Bible Study

10 COMMANDMENTS

1	2	3
4	5	6
7	8	9
10		

Lamplighters' 10 Commandments are proven small group leadership principles that have been used successfully to train hundreds of believers to lead life-changing, intentional discipleship Bible studies.

Essential Principles for Leading Intentional Discipleship Bible Studies

1. The 1st Commandment: The _____ Rule.
   The Leader-Trainer should be in the room _____ minutes before the class begins.

2. The 2nd Commandment: The _____-_____ Rule.
   Train the group that it is okay to _____, but they should never be
   _____.

3. The 3rd Commandment: The _____ Rule.
   _____, _____, _____ ask for
   _____ to _____ the _____, _____, and _____
   the questions. The Leader-Trainer, however, should always _____ the
   questions to control the _____ of the study.

4. The 4th Commandment: The ____:____ Rule.
   _____ the Bible study on time and _____ the study on time
   _____ _____. No exceptions!

5. The 5th Commandment: The _____ Rule.
   Train the group participants to _____ on God's Word for answers
   to life's questions.

1	2	3
4 **59:59**	5	6
7	8	9
	10	

6. The 6th Commandment: The _____ Rule.
   Deliberately and progressively _____ _____ participants into the
   group discussion over a period of time.

7. The 7th Commandment: The _____ _____ Rule.
   _____ the participants to get _____ the answers to the
   questions, not just _____ or _____ ones.

8. The 8th Commandment: The _____ Rule.
   _____ the group discussion so you _____ the
   lesson _____ _____ and give each question _____
   _____.

9. The 9th Commandment: The _____-_____ Rule.
   Don't let the group members talk about _____
   _____, _____ _____, or
   _____ _____.

10. The 10th Commandment: The _____ Rule.
    _____ God to change lives, including _____.

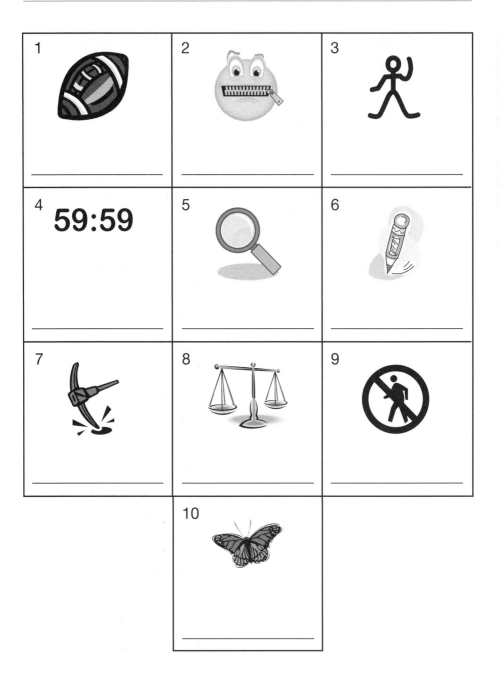

Choose your next study from any of the following titles:

- Joshua 1-9
- Joshua 10-24
- Judges 1-10
- Judges 11-21
- Ruth/Esther
- Jonah/Habakkuk
- Nehemiah
- Proverbs 1-9
- Proverbs 10-31
- Ecclesiastes
- John 1-11
- John 12-21
- Acts 1-12
- Acts 13-28

- Romans 1-8
- Romans 9-16
- Galatians
- Ephesians
- Philippians
- Colossians
- 1 & 2 Thessalonians
- 1 Timothy
- 2 Timothy
- Titus/Philemon
- Hebrews
- James
- 1 Peter
- 2 Peter/Jude

Additional Bible studies and sample lessons
are available online.

For audio introductions on all Bible studies,
visit us online at www.Lamplightersusa.org.

Looking to begin a new group?
The Lamplighters Starter Kit includes:

- 8 James Bible Study Guides
  (students purchase their own books)
- 25 Welcome Booklets
- 25 Table Tents
- 25 Bible Book Locator Bookmarks
- 50 Final Exam Tracts
- 50 Invitation Cards

For a current listing of live and online discipleship training
events, or to register for discipleship training, go to
www.LamplightersUSA.org/training.

Become a Certified Disciple-Maker

Discipleship Training Institute

Certificate of Completion

This is to certify that _____

has successfully completed the requirements of the

_____ course.

_____   _____
Date   President

Training Courses Available:

- Leader-Trainer
- Discipleship Coach
- Discipleship Director

Contact the Discipleship Training Institute for more information (800-507-9516).

The Discipleship Training Institute is a ministry of Lamplighters International.